THE SCHOOL MATHEMA⁊ PROJECT

When the SMP was founded in 1961, its main objec new secondary school mathematics courses to refl‗‗, ‗‗‗‗ ‗‗‗‗‗‗‗‗, ‗‗‗‗ did the traditional syllabuses, the up-to-date nature and usages of mathematics. The first texts produced embodied new courses for O-level (*SMP Books 1–5*) and A-level (*SMP Advanced Mathematics Books 1–4*). *Books 3, 4* and *5* have now been revised to become *SMP New Book 3, Parts 1* and *2, New Book 4, Parts 1* and *2,* and *New Book 5,* while *Revised Advanced Mathematics Books 1, 2* and *3* cover the syllabus for the A-level examination in SMP Mathematics. Five shorter texts cover the material of the various sections of the A-level examination SMP Further Mathematics. There are two books for SMP Additional Mathematics at O-level. All the SMP GCE examinations are available to schools through any of the GCE examining boards.

Books A–H cover broadly the same development of mathematics as the first few books of the O-level series. Most CSE boards offer appropriate examinations. In practice this series is being used very widely across all streams of comprehensive schools and its first seven books, together with *Books X, Y* and *Z,* provide a course leading to the SMP O-level examination. *SMP Cards I* and *II* provide an alternative treatment in card form of the mathematics in *Books A–D.* The six Units of *SMP 7–13,* designed for children in that age-range, provide a course for middle schools which is also widely used in primary schools and the first two years of secondary schools. *SMP 11–16,* the latest SMP course, provides the basis for a differentiated curriculum in the secondary school, catering for most children, including the most able. Teacher's Guides accompany all these series.

The SMP has produced many other texts and teachers are encouraged to obtain each year from Cambridge University Press, The Edinburgh Building, Shaftesbury Road, Cambridge CB2 2RU, the full list of SMP publications currently available. In the same way, help and advice may always be sought by teachers from the Executive Director at the SMP Office, Westfield College, Kidderpore Avenue, London NW3 7ST. SMP syllabuses and other information may be obtained from the same address.

The SMP is continually evaluating old work and preparing for new. The effectiveness of the SMP's work depends, as it has always done, on the comments and reactions received from a wide variety of teachers – and also from pupils – using SMP materials. Readers of the texts can, therefore, send their comments to the SMP in the knowledge that they will be valued and carefully studied.

ACKNOWLEDGEMENTS

The principal authors, on whose contributions the S.M.P. texts are largely based, are named in the annual Reports. Many other authors have also provided original material, and still more have been directly involved in the revision of draft versions of chapters and books. The Project gratefully acknowledges the contributions which they and their schools have made.

This book—*Book F*—has been written by

A. J. Dawkins	K. Lewis
Joyce Harris	R. W. Strong
D. A. Hobbs	Thelma Wilson

and edited by Elizabeth Smith.

The Project owes a great deal to its Secretaries, Miss Jacqueline Sinfield and Mrs Jennifer Whittaker, for their careful typing and assistance in connection with this book.

We would especially thank Professor J. V. Armitage for the advice he has given on the fundamental mathematics of the course.

The Project is grateful to International Computers Limited for supplying the photograph of a computer system at the head of Chapter 12.

Some of the drawings at the chapter openings in this book are by Ken Vail.

We are much indebted to the Cambridge University Press for their cooperation and help at all times.

THE SCHOOL MATHEMATICS PROJECT

BOOK F

CAMBRIDGE UNIVERSITY PRESS

Cambridge
London   New York   New Rochelle
Melbourne   Sydney

Published by the Press Syndicate of the University of Cambridge
The Pitt Building, Trumpington Street, Cambridge CB2 1RP
32 East 57th Street, New York, NY 10022, USA
296 Beaconsfield Parade, Middle Park, Melbourne 3206, Australia

Library of Congress catalogue card number: 68–21399

ISBN 0 521 08015 0 paperback
ISBN 0 521 08361 3 hard covers

First published 1970
Ninth printing 1983

Printed in Great Britain at the
University Press, Cambridge

Preface

This is the sixth of eight books primarily designed to cover a course suitable for those pupils who wish to take a C.S.E. examination on one of the reformed mathematics syllabuses.

By now, most of the topics to be studied in this course have already been introduced. We are convinced that it is very important for mathematics to be seen as a united subject and not as a collection of independent topics such as arithmetic, algebra, geometry and trigonometry. In this book we continue to show the links that exist between the various topics and the dependence of one on the other. For example, following the chapter on matrix multiplication in *Book E*, there are three chapters showing applications of this operation: the first is concerned with networks and is a sequel to Chapter 7, *Book C*; the second chapter deals with relations and extends work originally introduced in *Book B*, while the third shows how transformations can be described by matrices and ties in with the work done on transformations in Chapter 3 of this book and in earlier books.

Simple flow diagrams need no explanation: in fact, they generally clarify the situation. For this reason, we have already used flow diagrams on many different occasions in this course. The Prelude on flow diagrams introduces the use of question boxes and encourages clear thought by providing practice in working through practical and numerical flow diagrams and by encouraging pupils to construct flow diagrams of both types for themselves. There are three chapters in *Book F* which make use of flow diagrams: Formulas, Solutions of Equations and Computers and Programming. In the latter chapter we try to illustrate, in the most elementary way, what a computer can do and how it does it and also to show how problems can be broken down into series of simple logical steps. We include not only straightforward programs, but also those which involve loops, as such programs are a natural extension of the Prelude's work on flow diagrams with loops. The chapter on equations uses pairs of simple flow diagrams to explain the necessary steps for solving equations of the form $a - bx = c$, both by the method of inverse operations and by the method of inverse elements.

Chapter 2 takes a look at the many patterns that can be found among recurring decimals, while at the same time providing practice in division and changing fractions to decimals. The numerical work on lengths, areas and volumes of similar objects is kept simple and builds on the work done in the enlargement and ratio chapters in *Book D*. The computation in the trigonometry chapter in *Book F* is also kept as simple as possible. Chapter 4 introduces the words sine and cosine and explains how to use 3-figure tables but, like the chapter in *Book E*, it deals, for the time being, only with triangles in the first quadrant.

The chapter, Problems and their Solution Sets, revises and extends previous work on orderings and regions and prepares the way for the linear programming chapter in *Book H*. There is another statistics chapter in *Book F* and this one explains how to find the mean from a frequency table and how to estimate the mean from a grouped frequency table. The chapter includes a comparison of the results of grouping data in different ways.

Answers to exercises are not printed at the end of this book but are contained in the companion Teacher's Guide which gives a detailed commentary on the pupil's text. In this series, the answers and commentary are interleaved with the text.

Contents

Contents

Prelude

---

1. FLOW DIAGRAMS

Here is a puzzle for you to think about:

An army is on the march and comes to the left bank of a deep, crocodile-infested river. There is only one small boat available belonging to two boys. The boat is just big enough to carry the two boys alone or one soldier by himself.

How does the army get across to the right bank? (No ropes or other devices are allowed.)

You have ten minutes to solve this puzzle. Don't turn over until either you have solved it or the time is up.

Solution

The two boys row across to the right bank.

One of them gets out and the other one rows back.

He gets out, a soldier gets in, and rows across.

The soldier gets out and the boy rows back.

One soldier has now been transferred and the boys are back to their original position.

The whole procedure is then repeated until each member of the army has been transported across the river.

Another method of writing out the solution is by using a *flow diagram*. Look at the next page.

Follow the flow of the arrows.

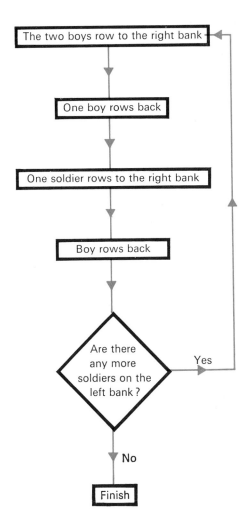

You will see that one 'box' is drawn differently from the others. It contains a question, and has two 'branches' coming out of it—'yes' and 'no'. If the answer is 'yes', then you go round the 'loop', and the procedure is repeated.

You will find some more problems with loops on the following pages.

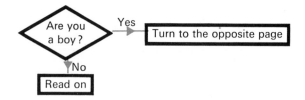

In a knitting pattern for a pullover the instructions for knitting part of the rib start as follows:

Using No. 10 needles cast on 65 sts.
1st row   Sl.1, K.1, * P.1, K.1, repeat from * to the last stitch, K.1.
2nd row   Sl.1, * P.1, K.1, repeat from * to end of row.

Here is a flow diagram for these instructions. Two of the boxes have been left blank. What should go in them?

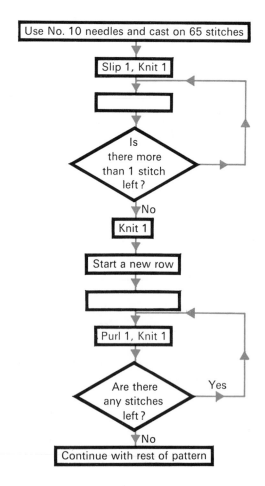

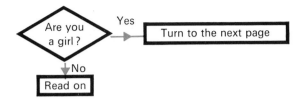

Here is a flow diagram showing you how to mix concrete. Two of the boxes have been left blank. What should go in them?

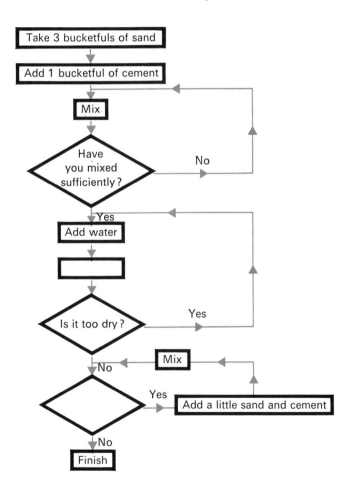

2. FLOW DIAGRAMS AND COMPUTERS

Computers can deal with very complicated problems, but before they can get down to work the problems have to be split up into easy steps. The first stage is to draw a flow diagram.

The diamond-shaped boxes containing questions in our flow diagrams have 'yes' or 'no' answers. This is because computers work on a 'yes' or 'no' system: if a light is on, it could mean 'yes'; if it is off, it could mean 'no'. Questions which have three possible answers such as 'yes' or 'no' or 'perhaps' are not allowed.

2.1 Drawing your own flow diagrams

Draw flow diagrams for some of the following situations. (Remember that when you use a diamond-shaped box for a question, the answer must be 'yes' or 'no'.)

1. The kerb drill: 'Look right, look left, look right again. Is the road clear? If it is, cross; if not, start again. (Your flow diagram should have one question box and one loop in it.)

2. Filling a bath. (Some question boxes you might want to include are 'Is it hot enough?', 'Is it full enough?'.)

3. Making a telephone call. (You might want to include question boxes such as 'Is the number engaged?', 'Is it the right number?'.)

4. Using a record player.

5. Using a tape recorder.

6. Starting a car.

7. Obtaining a drink out of a vending machine.

8. *Girls only.* Draw a flow diagram for the following knitting pattern:
    With No. 9 needles cast on 101 sts.

    1st row   *K.5, P.3, repeat from * to last 5 sts., K.5.
    2nd row   *P.5, K.3, repeat from * to last 5 sts., P.5.

9. *Boys only.* Draw a flow diagram for taking a penalty kick in football.

10. Make up a flow diagram for a subject of your own choice.

3. FLOW DIAGRAMS WITH NUMBERS

1. Work through the flow diagram in Figure 1.

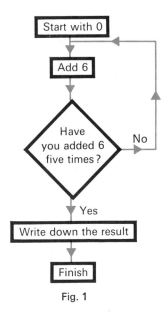

Fig. 1

(*a*) What does this flow diagram do?

(*b*) If you know how to use a calculating machine, explain the application of the flow diagram to a calculating machine.

(*c*) Write out a diagram of the same type for multiplying 9 by 8.

2. Work through the flow diagram in Figure 2.

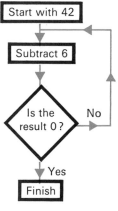

Fig. 2

(*a*) How many times did you subtract 6?

(*b*) What does this flow diagram do?

(*c*) If you know how to use a calculating machine, explain the application of the flow diagram to a calculating machine.

(*d*) Write out a flow diagram for dividing 56 by 8.

(*e*) What would happen if you tried to divide 57 by 8 on your flow diagram? Try to modify the question box so that it would work.

3. Work through the flow diagram in Figure 3.

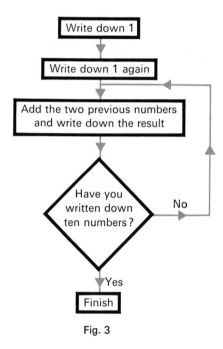

Fig. 3

You have met this set of numbers before. What is it called?

4. Work through the flow diagram in Figure 4 and name the set of numbers you obtain.

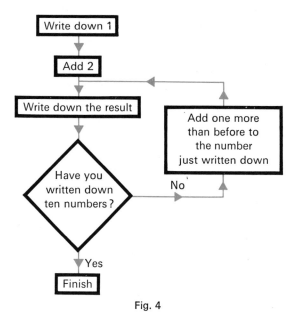

Fig. 4

5. Work through the flow diagram in Figure 5. What set of numbers do you obtain?

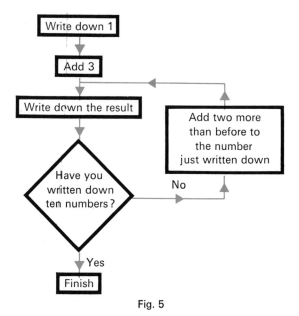

Fig. 5

6. Work through the flow diagram in Figure 6 and find out what it does.
Heights in centimetres: 164, 167, 161, 165, 163.

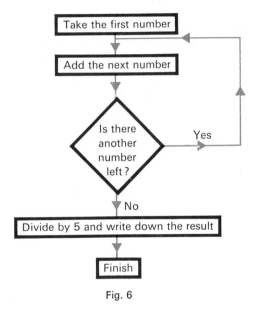

Fig. 6

7. Work through the flow diagram in Figure 7 and explain what it does.

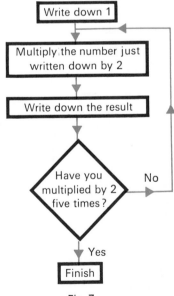

Fig. 7

8. Work through the flow diagram in Figure 8.

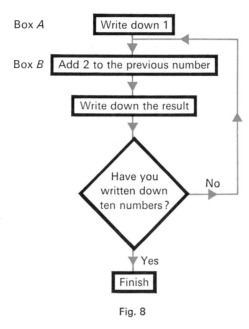

Fig. 8

(*a*) What set of numbers have you obtained?

(*b*) Alter Box A to obtain the first ten even numbers.

(*c*) Alter Box B to obtain the numbers 1, 4, 7, 10, 13, 16, 19, 22, 25, 28.

9. Construct a flow diagram to give the value of 3^6.

10. Construct a flow diagram to give the *sum* of the first ten counting numbers.

11. Invent a numerical flow diagram of your own choice.

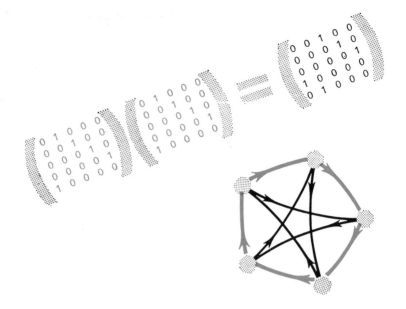

1. Matrices at work: networks

(a) Figure 1 (a) shows the network of roads linking the towns of Amfield, Benham and Colton. Copy and complete the matrix in Figure 1 (b) which describes this network.

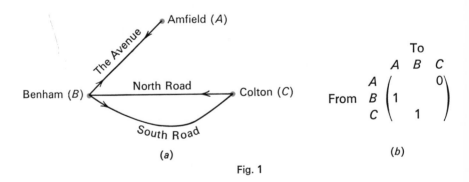

(a)

(b)

Fig. 1

Add the numbers in each row of the matrix. What do your answers tell you? Why?

A direct or 'one-stage' route is a journey which does not pass through another town or node on the way. Make a list of all the one-stage routes in the figure. How many are there?

Add all the numbers in the matrix. What does your answer tell you? Why?

Is there a one-stage route from (i) *A* to *C*; (ii) *A* to *A*?

We *can* travel from *A* to *C* if we first go from *A* to *B* and then from *B* to *C*. $A \rightarrow B \rightarrow C$ is a 'two-stage' route from *A* to *C*.

Is there a two-stage route from *A* to *A*? If so, which town would we pass through on the way?

Suppose we start at *A*. A one-stage journey would take us to *B*:

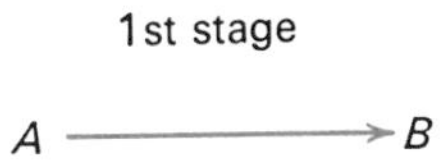

1st stage

$$A \longrightarrow B$$

From *B*, we can either return to *A* or go to *C*:

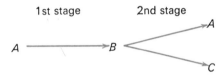

This shows that there is

   (i) a two-stage route which starts at *A* and finishes at *A*;
   (ii) a two-stage route which starts at *A* and finishes at *C*.

Is there a two-stage route which starts at *A* and finishes at *B*?

We can now complete the first row of a matrix which shows all the possible two-stage routes:

$$\begin{array}{c} & & \text{To} \\ & & A \quad B \quad C \\ \text{From} \begin{array}{c} A \\ B \\ C \end{array} & \begin{pmatrix} 1 & 0 & 1 \\ & & \\ & & \end{pmatrix} \end{array}$$

Fig. 2

Copy and complete the following diagram to show the two-stage routes which start at *B*:

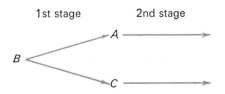

Draw a similar diagram to show the two-stage routes which start at *C*. Use your diagrams to help you to complete a copy of the two-stage route matrix in Figure 2.

The one-stage route matrix is

$$
\begin{array}{c c}
 & \begin{array}{c c c} A & B & C \end{array} \\
\begin{array}{c} A \\ B \\ C \end{array} &
\begin{pmatrix}
0 & 1 & 0 \\
1 & 0 & 1 \\
0 & 1 & 0
\end{pmatrix}
\end{array}
$$

and the two-stage route matrix is

$$
\begin{array}{c c}
 & \begin{array}{c c c} A & B & C \end{array} \\
\begin{array}{c} A \\ B \\ C \end{array} &
\begin{pmatrix}
1 & 0 & 1 \\
0 & 2 & 0 \\
1 & 0 & 1
\end{pmatrix}
\end{array}.
$$

Multiply the one-stage route matrix by itself, that is, work out

$$
\begin{array}{c c}
 & \begin{array}{c c c} A & B & C \end{array} \\
\begin{array}{c} A \\ B \\ C \end{array} &
\begin{pmatrix}
0 & 1 & 0 \\
1 & 0 & 1 \\
0 & 1 & 0
\end{pmatrix}
\end{array}
\begin{array}{c c}
 & \begin{array}{c c c} A & B & C \end{array} \\
\begin{array}{c} A \\ B \\ C \end{array} &
\begin{pmatrix}
0 & 1 & 0 \\
1 & 0 & 1 \\
0 & 1 & 0
\end{pmatrix}
\end{array}.
$$

Compare your answer with the two-stage route matrix.

It is interesting to note that multiplying a one-stage route matrix by itself gives the two-stage route matrix.

(*b*) During holiday periods the traffic along North Road is very heavy. The local county council proposes to widen South Road and to allow traffic to travel along this road in both directions (see Figure 3).

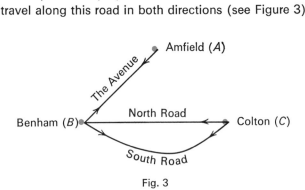

Fig. 3

Write down the matrix which describes the one-stage routes for the new network. Call it **R**.

Either list all the possible two-stage routes or draw diagrams to show them. You should be able to find two which start at *A*, three which start at *B* and four which start at *C*. Use your results to help you to write down the matrix which describes these two-stage routes. Call it **S**.

Multiply **R** by itself, that is, find **R**^{2}. Is it true that **S** = **R**^{2}?

(*c*) On an island there are only two towns, Alport and Hightown (see Figure 4). The island bus runs on two routes:

(i) between Alport and Hightown in both directions;
(ii) from Hightown through some small villages and back to Hightown.

Copy and complete the one-stage route matrix which describes these journeys. Call it **T**.

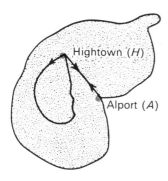

$$\mathbf{T} = \begin{array}{c} \\ A \\ H \end{array} \begin{array}{c} A \quad H \\ \left(\begin{array}{cc} & \\ & 1 \end{array} \right) \end{array}$$

Fig. 4

What is meant by the leading diagonal of a matrix? Why does the leading diagonal of **T** contain a number other than 0? When would it contain a 2?

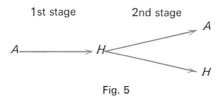

Fig. 5

The diagram in Figure 5 shows the possible two-stage routes which start at Alport. Draw a similar diagram to show those which start at Hightown.

Write down the two-stage route matrix and check that it is equal to **T**^{2}, that is, **T** multiplied by itself.

Find **T**^{3}. What information does this matrix give?

Exercise A

1 Write down the one-stage route matrix for the network in Figure 6. By multiplying the matrix by itself, find the two-stage route matrix. List these two-stage routes by tracing them in the diagram, for example, $A \rightarrow C \rightarrow B$ and so on.

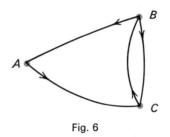

Fig. 6

2 Repeat Question 1 for the network in Figure 7.

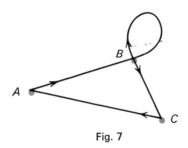

Fig. 7

3 Write down the one-stage route matrix for the network in Figure 8. Call it **R**. Multiply **R** by itself, that is, find R^2. How many two-stage routes are there?

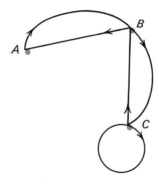

Fig. 8

4 Write down the one-stage route matrix for the network in Figure 9. Call it **S**. Find S^2. How many two-stage routes are there? Find S^3. How many three-stage routes are there?

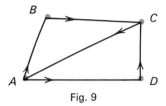

Fig. 9

5 Write down the one-stage route matrix for the network in Figure 10. Call it **T**. Find T^2 and explain why the first column of **T** and the first column of T^2 contain only 0's.

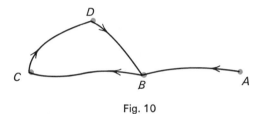

Fig. 10

6 Write down the one-stage route matrix for the network in Figure 11. Call it **U**. Find U^2, U^3, U^4 and U^5 and explain your result.

Fig. 11

7 Write down the one-stage route matrix for the network in Figure 12. Call it **V**. Find V^2, V^3, V^4, V^5, V^6, V^7. Describe any number patterns which you find in your answers.

Fig. 12

8 Draw a simple network of your own. Find the one- and two-stage matrices for your network.

9 Write down the one-stage route matrix for the network in Figure 13. Call it **W**. Find **W²** and **W⁴**. How many four-stage routes are there:

(a) starting and finishing at the same point;

(b) starting and finishing at different points?

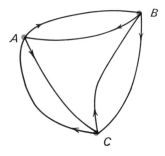

Fig. 13

10 The networks in Figure 14 have no direct routes from a node to itself and no more than one direct route between any two nodes.

Find the two-stage matrices for each of these networks. What do you notice about the numbers on the leading diagonals? Why do you think this happens?

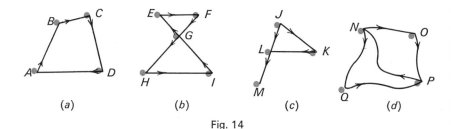

(a)   (b)   (c)   (d)

Fig. 14

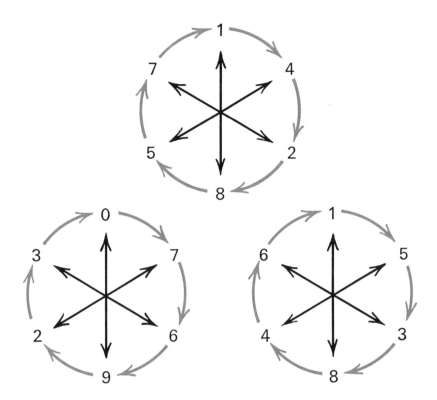

2. Patterns with decimals

(a) We can think of $\frac{3}{4}$ as 3 divided by 4.

$$4)\overline{3 \cdot 00}$$
$$\overline{0 \cdot 75}$$

So $\frac{3}{4} = 0 \cdot 75$.

Use this method to write the following fractions as decimals: (i) $\frac{1}{4}$; (ii) $\frac{3}{5}$; (iii) $\frac{1}{2}$; (iv) $\frac{5}{8}$.

(b) What happens when you try to write $\frac{1}{3}$ as a decimal?

$\frac{3}{4}, \frac{1}{4}, \frac{3}{5}, \frac{1}{2}, \frac{5}{8}$ can all be written as *terminating* decimals. For example, $\frac{3}{4}$ stops or terminates after two decimal places, but

$$\frac{1}{3} = 0 \cdot 3333333333\ldots!$$

The threes continue for ever to the right of the point. We write this number for short as $0 \cdot \dot{3}$.

The dot above the 3 shows that it is continually repeated.

19

Check that $\frac{5}{11} = 0\cdot45454545....$

This time *two* figures are repeated and we write

$$0\cdot45454545...\quad\text{as}\quad 0\cdot4\dot{5},$$

that is, we put a dot above the *first and last figures of the repeating group.* Here are some more examples:

$0\cdot3247247247247...$ is written as $0\cdot3\dot{2}4\dot{7}$, showing that 247 is repeated;

$0\cdot1637526375263752...$ is written as $0\cdot1\dot{6}375\dot{2}$, showing that 63752 is repeated.

Decimals with a repeating group of figures are called *recurring decimals.*

(c) What do you think is meant by (i) $0\cdot\dot{6}$, (ii) $4\cdot\dot{0}\dot{2}$, (iii) $3\cdot\dot{4}1\dot{7}$?

(d) Write in shorthand with dots above
  (i) $0\cdot36363636...$, (ii) $11\cdot11111...$, (iii) $4\cdot324324324324....$

(e) If we wish to write $\frac{1}{13}$ as a decimal, we must first divide 1 by 13:

$$\begin{array}{r} 0\cdot07692307...\ \hline 13)\overline{1\cdot00000000...} \\ 91 \\ \hline 90 \\ 78 \\ \hline 120 \\ 117 \\ \hline 30 \\ 26 \\ \hline 40 \\ 39 \\ \hline 100 \\ 91 \\ \hline \end{array}$$

So $\frac{1}{13} = 0\cdot\dot{0}7692\dot{3}$.

Use the method of long division to write $\frac{2}{13}$ as a decimal.

Exercise A

Questions 2, 3, 4, 5, 6 and 7 require a lot of arithmetic. You will save time if you work with two or three other people.

1 Write the following recurring decimals in shorthand with dots:

  (a) $0\cdot777777...$;   (b) $0\cdot424242...$;   (c) $0\cdot417417417...$;

  (d) $3\cdot466666...$;   (e) $4\cdot7989898...$;   (f) $6\cdot254254254...$;

  (g) $6\cdot464646...$;   (h) $8\cdot35747474...$;   (i) $3\cdot193193193...$;

  (j) $7\cdot64236423...$;   (k) $2\cdot4124121212...$;   (l) $363\cdot63636363....$

2 Write the following fractions as decimals:

$$\frac{1}{2}, \frac{1}{3}, \frac{1}{4}, \frac{1}{5}, \frac{1}{6}, \frac{1}{7}, \ldots, \frac{1}{19}, \frac{1}{20}, \frac{1}{21}.$$

You can add some more fractions to this list if you wish. Keep your results; you will need some of them again.

Which fractions can be written as terminating decimals? Try to find a general rule which the bottom numbers of these fractions must obey.

Does it make any difference to your answer if the top numbers are larger than 1?

3 Write the following fractions as decimals:

$$\frac{1}{7}, \frac{2}{7}, \frac{3}{7}, \frac{4}{7}, \frac{5}{7}, \frac{6}{7}.$$

How many figures recur in each of your answers?

Write about any number patterns which you notice.

4 Write the following fractions as decimals:

$$\frac{1}{11}, \frac{2}{11}, \frac{3}{11}, \frac{4}{11}, \frac{5}{11}, \frac{6}{11}, \frac{7}{11}, \frac{8}{11}, \frac{9}{11}, \frac{10}{11}.$$

How many figures recur in each of your answers?

Write briefly about any number patterns which you notice. Are the patterns for the elevenths similar to those for the sevenths?

5 We know that $\frac{1}{13} = 0 \cdot 0\dot{7}692\dot{3}$ and $\frac{2}{13} = 0 \cdot \dot{1}5384\dot{6}$.

Work out $\frac{3}{13}, \frac{4}{13}, \frac{5}{13}, \frac{6}{13}, \frac{7}{13}, \frac{8}{13}, \frac{9}{13}, \frac{10}{13}, \frac{11}{13}$ and $\frac{12}{13}$.

What number patterns do the thirteenths have? Are they like the patterns for the sevenths or the elevenths?

6 Express the seventeenths as recurring decimals and write about their number patterns.

7 Express the twenty-oneths as recurring decimals. Compare their number patterns with those of other fractions which you have investigated.

8 Write the following terminating decimals as fractions in their simplest form:

(a) 0·7;   (b) 2·5;   (c) 1·41;   (d) 1·42;

(e) 0·023;   (f) 10·6;   (g) 0·32;   (h) 9·75.

9 (a) Write down six fractions which can be written as terminating decimals.

(b) Write down six fractions which can be written as recurring decimals.

10 Can you see how the decimal 0·12112111211112... is being built up?

(a) Is it a terminating decimal?

(b) Is it a recurring decimal?

(c) Make up some more decimals like this.

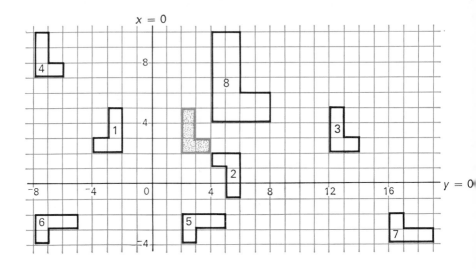

3. Combined transformations

1. TRANSFORMATIONS

(*a*) The red **L** in the figure above can be mapped or *transformed* onto **L1** by a reflection. What is the equation of the mirror line?

(*b*) The red **L** can be transformed onto **L2** by a rotation. Where is the centre of this rotation? What is the angle of the rotation?

(*c*) The red **L** can be transformed onto **L3** by a translation. What is the vector of this translation?

(*d*) Describe how the red **L** can be transformed onto each of the other **L**'s. More than one transformation may be required in one case.

(*e*) Which of the transformations you have just used do you think is the 'odd one out'? Explain why you think so.

Exercise A

Copy Figure 1 onto squared paper. You will need it for the first five questions in this exercise.

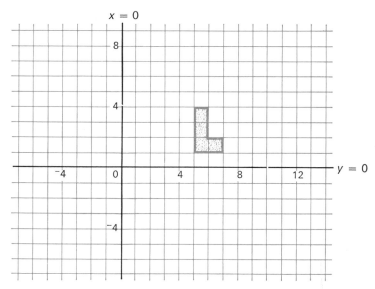

Fig. 1

1 Translate the red **L** in Figure 1 by the vector $\begin{pmatrix} 3 \\ 2 \end{pmatrix}$. Label the new position **L**1. Then translate **L**1 by $\begin{pmatrix} 4 \\ 3 \end{pmatrix}$ and label it **L**2. What single transformation would map **L**2 back onto the original **L**?

2 Reflect the original **L** in the line $y = 0$. Call the new position **L**3. Reflect **L**3 in the line $x = 0$ to give **L**4.
   What single transformation would map **L**4 back onto the original **L**?

3 (*a*) Reflect the original **L** in the line $y = x$. (You may need tracing paper to help you.) Call the new position **L**5. What is the inverse of this reflection, that is, what transformation would map **L**5 back onto the original **L**?
   (*b*) Reflect the original **L** in the line $y = {}^-x$. Call the new position **L**6. What is the inverse of this reflection?

4 Rotate the original **L** through 90° anticlockwise about (0, 0). Call the new position **L**7.
   Rotate **L**7 through 180° anticlockwise about (0, 0) to give **L**8.
   What single transformation would map **L**8 back onto the original **L**?

23

5   Reflect the original **L** in the line $x = 3$. Call the new position **L9**.
Reflect **L9** in the line $x = ^-2$ to give **L10**.
What single transformation would map **L10** back onto the original **L**?

6   On squared paper draw axes in the middle of the page and draw the
lines $y = x$ and $y = ^-x$. Join up the points (2, 1), (7, 1), (7, 4) to
form a triangle. Label it *A*.
Reflect *A* in the line $y = x$ to give triangle *B*.
Reflect *B* in the line $x = 0$ to give triangle *C*.
Reflect *C* in the line $y = ^-x$ to give triangle *D*.
Reflect *D* in the line $y = 0$ to give triangle *E*.
Continue this process until the triangle is back to *A*. Describe single
transformations which would map

(*a*) *A* onto *E*;   (*b*) *B* onto *G*;

(*c*) *D* onto *H*;   (*d*) *E* onto *B*.

7   Figure 2 shows the reflection of an **L** in a mirror line. What can be said
about the angles marked *p* and *q*?

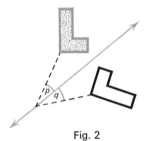

Fig. 2

In Figure 3, another mirror line has been added, and the new **L** has
been reflected in it. What can you say about the angles marked *r* and *s*?
Describe a single transformation which would map the final **L** back
to its original position.

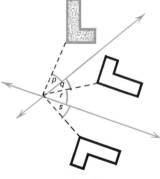

Fig. 3

24

8 Describe the transformations which map the red **L** in Figure 4 onto each of the other **L**'s. How do these transformations differ from reflections, rotations and translations?

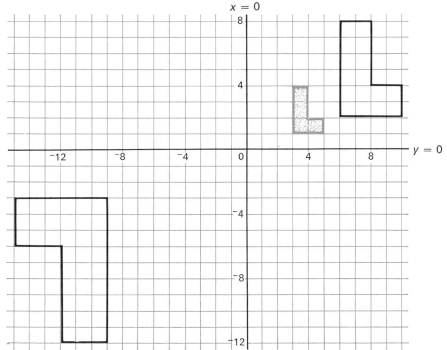

Fig. 4

9 What combination of transformations would map the red **L** in Figure 5 onto **L1**?

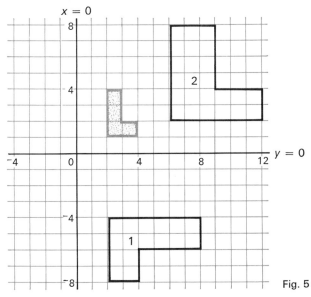

Fig. 5

10 How could the red **L** in Figure 5 be mapped onto **L2**?

11 On squared paper draw a shape of your own. Choose a non-symmetrical shape and do not make it too complicated.

Make up some questions like those in this exercise involving transformations. Answer them yourself, and then try them out on your neighbour.

2. REFLECTIONS IN PARALLEL MIRRORS

(These are *mathematical* mirrors, with special properties rather different from ordinary mirrors.)

Six people are needed for this.

First Mirror	(A mirror is represented by someone standing with arms outstretched.)
Second Mirror	
Chief Pacer	(His job is to measure distances by pacing out.)
Object	
First Image	
Second Image.	

The mirrors take up their positions standing with their arms outstretched parallel to each other 5 paces apart (measured by the Chief Pacer).

The Object stands 2 paces, say, from the First Mirror (see Figure 6).

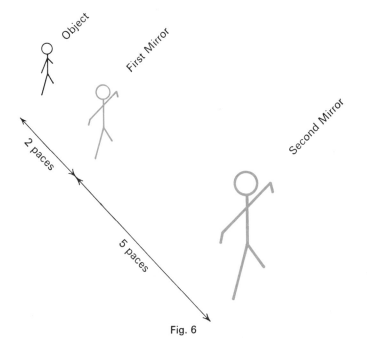

Fig. 6

The First Image then moves into position—he is the reflection of the Object in the First Mirror.

The Second Image stands in the correct position for the reflection of the First Image in the Second Mirror (see Figure 7).

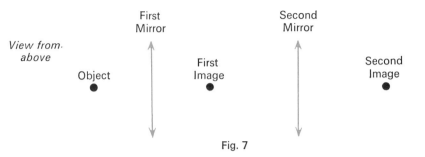

Fig. 7

The scene is now set. Try these:

(a) The Object stands on his right leg only. What do the Images do?

(b) The Object holds his right ear with his right hand. What do the Images do?

(c) The Object moves his right hand over his head in a clockwise direction. What do the Images do?

(d) How many paces apart are the Object and the Second Image?

(e) The Object takes one pace away from the First Mirror. The two Images move into their correct positions. How far apart are the Object and the Second Image now?

(f) The Object takes two paces towards the First Mirror. The two Images move into their correct positions. How far apart are the Object and the Second Image now?

(g) The two Mirrors now stand 4 paces apart. Repeat Questions (d), (e) and (f).

There is a relation between the distance from the Object to the Second Image and the distance between the Mirrors. Can you spot it?

If not, try some more experiments with different distances between the Mirrors.

You may suspect that the distance between the Object and the Second Image is twice the distance between the Mirrors. On the next page there is a method for showing that this is true.

Call the distance from the Object to the First Mirror *a* (see Figure 8).

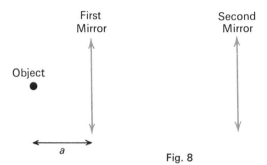

Fig. 8

Figure 9 shows the first reflection. What can be said about the distance indicated by the dotted arrow?

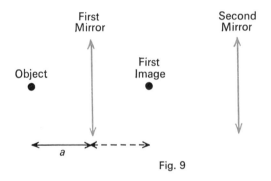

Fig. 9

Call the distance from the First Image to the Second Mirror *b* (see Figure 10). What can be said about the distance indicated by the dotted arrow?

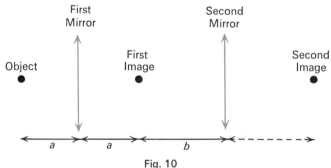

Fig. 10

You should now be able to see that the total distance from the Object to the Second Image is always twice the distance between the Mirrors.

Look back at your solution to Exercise *A*, Question 5 and check that your answer there agrees with this result.

2.1   Some further investigations

1. Does the same result apply if the Object starts off *between* the Mirrors?

2. What happens if the reflections are carried out in the opposite order, that is, reflection in the Second Mirror first?

2.2   Making patterns

(*a*) On squared paper, draw two mirror lines about 5 cm apart.
Draw an object—choose one which is not symmetrical. Figure 11 shows an example.

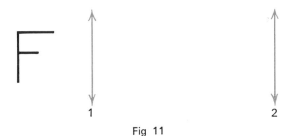

Fig 11

Reflect first in Mirror 1, and then reflect the image in Mirror 2.
(i)   How far apart are the object and the second image?
(ii) What single transformation would map the object onto the second image?

(*b*) Now reflect the second image in Mirror 1, and then reflect this new image in Mirror 2, and so on. Make as many reflections as you can until you cannot get any more on your page.

(*c*) Figure 12 shows a wallpaper border pattern. It can be made by reflections, as you have just done in (*b*). Design an interesting shape and make a wallpaper border pattern of your own.

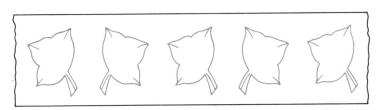

Fig. 12

3. REFLECTIONS IN INTERSECTING MIRRORS

(*a*) You will need a piece of tracing paper for this.

Make two folds intersecting at an angle of about 60° (it need not be accurately 60°). The folds represent mirror lines.

Draw an object in roughly the position shown in Figure 13. Any object will do, but do not make it too complicated.

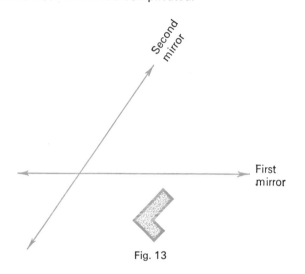

Fig. 13

Reflect the object in the first mirror by folding the tracing paper, and copying the object through.

Now reflect this image in the second mirror.

Look at the object and the second image. What single transformation would map the object onto the second image? (You might find it helpful in answering this to put another piece of tracing paper on top of the first piece and trace the object through.)

(*b*) In Figure 14, an angle has been marked *a*. What can be said about the angle indicated by the dotted arrow?

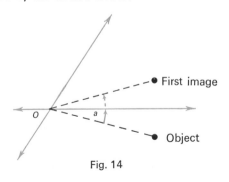

Fig. 14

Figure 15 shows the second image also. What can be said about the angle indicated by the dotted arrow?

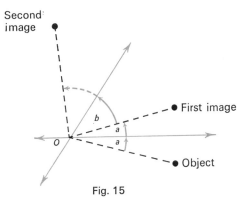

Fig. 15

Explain how this shows that the two reflections are equivalent to a rotation about *O* through twice the angle between the mirrors.

Did you come to the same conclusion in your tracing paper experiment? Look back at your solution to Exercise A, Question 7.

3.1 Some further investigations

1. Does the same result apply if the object starts off *between* the mirrors?

2. What happens if the reflections are carried out in the opposite order, that is, reflection in the second mirror first?

3. You can try using people for showing reflections in intersecting mirrors in the same way that you did for parallel mirrors. It is more difficult to do because it is not as easy to get the angles correct as it was to get the distances correct.

3.2 Making a kaleidoscope

You will need:
　　　　　　　two pocket mirrors,
　　　　　　　a protractor.

Hold the mirrors vertically over a horizontal protractor as in Figure 16 (over page).

Put some small pieces of coloured paper between the mirrors.

Look in the mirrors at the images. By changing the angle between the mirrors you will be able to change the number of images.

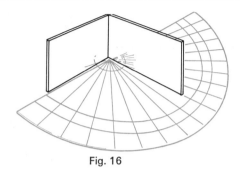

Fig. 16

To see how a kaleidoscope works, draw two lines on a piece of tracing paper intersecting at an angle of 60° (see Figure 17).

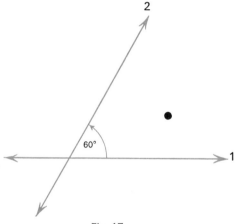

Fig. 17

Mark a point between the mirrors. Find the reflection of this point in Mirror 1. (The easiest way is to fold the paper.) Reflect the image in Mirror 2. Then reflect the new image in Mirror 1, and so on.

You should find that eventually the image comes back to the position of the object.

Repeat with an angle of 45°.

Now try angles of 72° and 50°.

Try to explain the results you obtain.

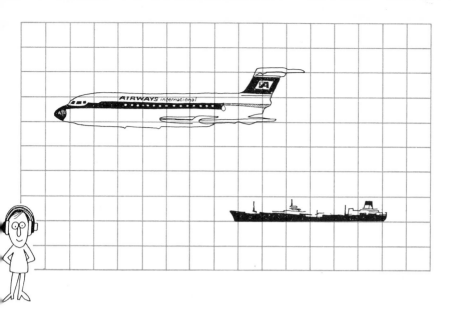

4. Trigonometry

1. TRIGONOMETRY

(a) The word *trigonometry* may be new to you. Trigonometry is concerned with the measurement of angles. You have done some trigonometry before: perhaps this table of coordinates will remind you.

Angle	x	y
10°	0·99	0·17
20°	0·94	0·34
30°	0·87	0·50
40°	0·77	0·64
→ 50°	0·64	0·77
60°	.0·50	0·87
70°	0·34	0·94
80°	0·17	0·99

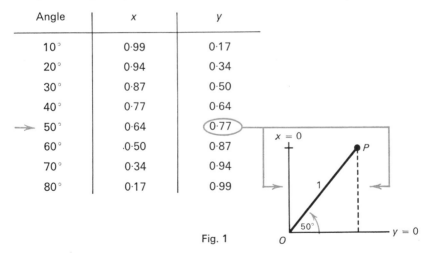

Fig. 1

This table tells you that, for example, the y-coordinate of P in Figure 1 is 0·77.

What is the x-coordinate of P?

(*b*) Figure 2 is obtained from Figure 1 by an enlargement, centre O, scale factor 3.

The y-coordinate of Q is $0{\cdot}77 \times 3$, that is $2{\cdot}31$.

What is the x-coordinate of Q?

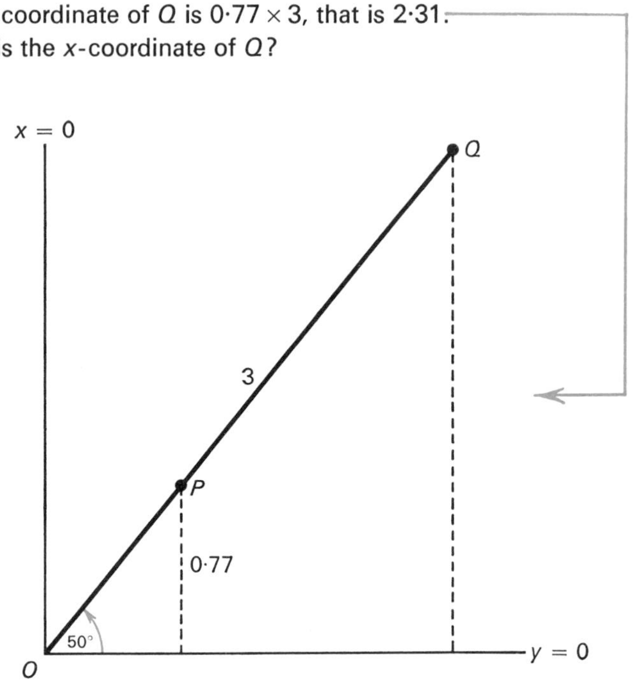

x = 0
Q
3
P
0·77
50°
O
y = 0

Fig. 2

(*c*) Here is a problem from *Book E*:

A 20 m ladder leans against the wall of a house so that the angle between the ladder and the ground is 50°. How far is the foot of the ladder from the wall?

Figure 3 is a rough diagram of the situation and alongside it are the coordinates for 50° obtained from the table at the beginning of this chapter.

Wall
20
50°
Scale
factor
20
1
0·77
50°
O
0·64

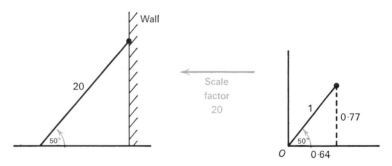

Fig. 3

The scale factor of the required enlargement is 20.
Hence the distance from the foot of the ladder to the wall is 0·64 × 20 m, that is 12·8 m.
What is the height of the top of the ladder above ground level?

Exercise A

1   Find the *x*- and *y*-coordinates of the points *A*, *B* and *C* in Figure 4.

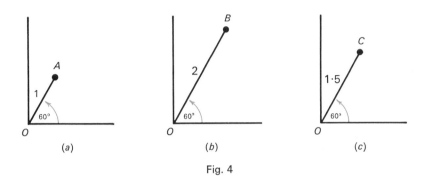

Fig. 4

In each of the following questions draw a rough diagram of the situation and alongside it draw a small diagram as in Figure 3 showing the coordinates.

2   A road rises at 10° to the horizontal for 400 m. What is the gain in height in walking along it?

3   An aeroplane is climbing at an angle of 30° to the horizontal. What is its increase in height when it has gone 2000 m?

4   The jib of a crane is 25 m long and is inclined at 80° to the horizontal. How high is the top of the jib above its base?

5   In a game of hockey the ball is hit a distance of 17 m at an angle of 40° to the side line. How far does it go up the field? How far does it go across the field?

6   A ship sails 87 km on a bearing of 020°. What angle does its course make with the east–west direction? How far north is the ship from its original position? How far east?

2. SINES AND COSINES

The table at the beginning of this chapter gives the coordinates for certain angles only. In order to obtain the coordinates for an angle such as 32·5° you will need a bigger table such as the one in the S.M.P. Elementary Tables. You will find the required information on pages 4 and 5 under the heading *cosine* (corresponding to the *x*-coordinates in our table) and on pages 2 and 3 under the heading *sine* (corresponding to the *y*-coordinates in our table).

> cosine gives the *x*-coordinate
>
> sine   gives the *y*-coordinate

Here is how to use the tables.

To find the sine of 30° look down the left-hand side of page 2 until you come to 30. Read off the answer in the next column (the heading ·0 to that column means that you are looking up 30·0°). Check that this agrees with the table at the beginning of this chapter.

To find the sine of 30·4°, put your finger on 30 in the left-hand column and read across to the column headed ·4. You should find 0·506.

What is the sine of 30·7°?

For the cosines, turn to pages 4 and 5 of the tables.

What is the cosine of 40°?

What is the cosine of 40·8°?

You will find that the sine and cosine tables are more accurate than the table of coordinates at the beginning of this chapter. They give the sines and cosines correct to 3 decimal places. But they are not exact—they are only approximately correct. However, 3 decimal places are usually sufficient for most practical purposes. It is possible to have more accurate tables—4 figures and 7 figures are used when appropriate.

It is important that you should be able to use the tables quickly and accurately. Exercise B is intended to give you practice.

Exercise B

1 Find the sines of the following angles:

    (*a*) 27·0°;   (*b*) 27·5°;   (*c*) 27·7°;

    (*d*) 81·2°;   (*e*) 57·1°;   (*f*) 39·4°.

2 Find the cosines of the following angles:

    (*a*) 42·8°;   (*b*) 51·3°;   (*c*) 8·1°;

    (*d*) 90·0°;   (*e*) 60·0°;   (*f*) 4·2°.

3 Find the angles whose sines are:

   (*a*) 0·918;   (*b*) 0·047;   (*c*) 0·640.

4 Find the angles whose cosines are:

   (*a*) 0·191;   (*b*) 0·700;   (*c*) 0·936.

5 (*a*) Find the sine of 40°.
   Subtract 40° from 90°, to give 50°, and look up the cosine of 50°.

   (*b*) Find the sine of 25°.
   Subtract 25° from 90°, and look up the cosine of this angle.

   (*c*) Find the sine of 37·6°.
   Subtract 37·6° from 90° and look up the cosine of this angle.

   (*d*) What do you notice in (*a*), (*b*) and (*c*)?

   (*e*) What is the relation between the sine of $a°$ and the cosine of $90° - a°$? Why?

6 What is the greatest value the sine of an angle, or the cosine of an angle, can have? Why?

7 Figure 5 (*a*) shows a wheel. The red spoke started in a horizontal position and has rotated through an angle $a°$. Suppose that the radius of the wheel is 1 unit, then the height of the point *P* above its original position is the sine of $a°$.

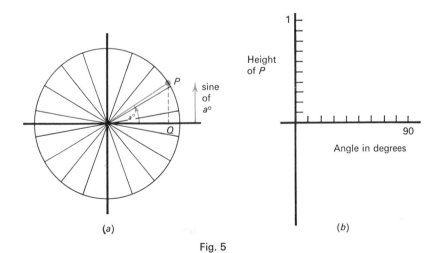

Fig. 5

Complete the table on p. 38 by looking up the sines of the angles, and hence draw a graph (see Figure 5 (*b*)) showing how the height of *P* varies.

Angle ($a°$)	Height of P
0	
10	
20	
30	
40	
50	
60	
70	
80	
90	

8 Use the same sheet of graph paper as in Question 7 and with another colour, draw a graph showing the horizontal distance of Q from the centre of the wheel, that is, the cosine of $a°$.

What do you notice about the two curves?

9 See what you can find out about the origins of the words—sine and cosine.

3. SOLVING PROBLEMS WITH THE SINE AND COSINE TABLES

Just a reminder:

> The cosine corresponds to the x-coordinate;
> the sine corresponds to the y-coordinate.

It may help to remember that the alphabetical order is the same: c comes before s, x comes before y.

Here is a problem which can be solved using the tables:

An aeroplane climbs at an angle of $42·7°$ to the horizontal. What is its increase in height after going 500 m?

Figure 6 is a rough diagram of the situation, and alongside it is a diagram showing the coordinates for $42·7°$ obtained from the tables.

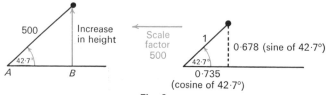

Fig. 6

The required scale is 500. Hence the aeroplane's increase in height is

$$0 \cdot 678 \times 500 \text{ m,}$$

which is 339 m.

Using the cosine of 42·7°, find how far the aeroplane has travelled over the ground, that is, the distance *AB*.

Exercise C

In each of these questions draw a rough diagram of the situation and alongside draw a small diagram as in Figure 6 showing the coordinates obtained from the sine and cosine tables.

1 Find the *x*- and *y*-coordinates of the points *P*, *Q* and *R* in Figure 7.

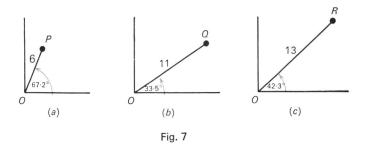

Fig. 7

2 A see-saw is 4 m long and is inclined at 22° to the horizontal. How much higher is the upper end than the lower end?

3 An escalator in a large store is 17 m long and makes an angle of 33·4° with the horizontal. What is the distance between the two floor levels?

4 A diagonal of a rectangle is 4 cm long and makes an angle of 54·8° with one side. Find the length and width of the rectangle.

5 A ship sails 119 km on a *bearing* of 047·9°. How far north is it from its original position?
    The ship then alters course to 032·7° for 53 km. What further distance has it gone north?
    What is the ship's total distance north of its original position?
    Find the ship's total distance east of its original position.

6 An aeroplane flies 211 km on a bearing of 024·5° and then changes to a bearing of 058·3° for 155 km.
    Find the aeroplane's total distances north and east of its original position.

4. FINDING ANGLES

(*a*) In Figure 8, *OP* is of length 2 and the *y*-coordinate of *P* is 1·638.
Problem: calculate the size of angle *a*.

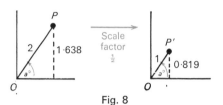

Fig. 8

This can be done by enlarging, or rather reducing, *OP* until it is of length 1, as shown.

The required scale factor is ½, and the *y*-coordinate of *P'* is then 1·638 × ½, that is 0·819.

Look up 0·819 in your sine tables and hence find the size of angle *a*.

(*b*) In Figure 9, *OQ* is of length 3, and the *x*-coordinate of *Q* is 2·157.

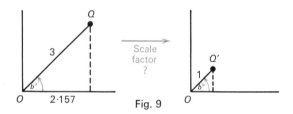

Fig. 9

In order to make *OQ'* of length 1, what would the scale factor of the enlargement (reduction) be?

What then would be the *x*-coordinate of *Q'*?

Use your cosine tables to find the size of angle *b*.

(*c*) A ladder of length 12 m is leaning against a wall and the top of it is 10 m above the ground (see Figure 10). It is required to find the angle of inclination of the ladder to the ground.

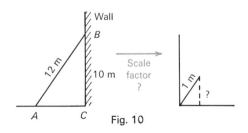

Fig. 10

Imagine an enlargement (reduction) to take place so that the length *AB* becomes 1 m as shown. What would be the scale factor of the enlargement?

What would the length of *BC* become? Hence find the angle of inclination of the ladder.

Exercise D

1 In Figure 11, *OP* maps onto *OP'* under an enlargement with scale factor ¼. Find the *y*-coordinate of *P'*. Hence find the size of *a*.

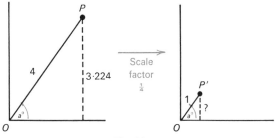

Fig. 11

2 In Figure 12, *OQ* maps onto *OQ'* under an enlargement with scale factor ⅕. Find the *x*-coordinate of *Q'*. Hence find the size of *b*.

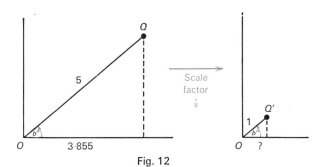

Fig. 12

In each of the following questions draw a rough diagram of the situation and alongside draw an enlarged (or reduced) diagram, as in Figures 11 and 12.

3   In Figure 13, find the sizes of the lettered angles.

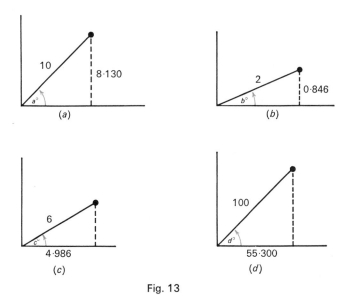

Fig. 13

4   A road slopes steadily upwards, and there is a gain of height of 15·1 m in travelling 100 m along the road. What is the angle of slope?

5   An aeroplane increases its height by 319 m after climbing for 1000 m. What is the angle of climb?

6   A ship sails on a straight course for a distance of 200 km from port and in so doing, its final distance east of the port is 23·6 km. Find the ship's bearing.

7   A mountain railway rises vertically 102 m in 300 m of track length. What is the angle of the track?

8   A ladder 10 m long leans against a wall and the foot is 5·42 m from the wall. Find the angle of slope of the ladder.

9   The tops of two posts of heights 4 m and 9 m are joined by a wire 20 m long. What is the angle of slope of the wire?

5. FINDING LENGTHS

(*a*) In Figure 14 (*a*), the *x*-coordinate of *P* is 5, and *OP* makes an angle of 60° with the *y* = 0 axis.

Problem: find the length of *OP*.

The information shown in Figure 14 (*b*) was obtained by looking up 60° in cosine tables.

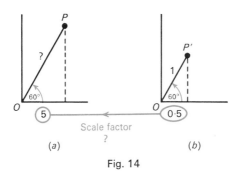

(*a*)   (*b*)

Fig. 14

What scale factor would convert 0·5 into 5? Hence find the length of *OP*.

(*b*) In Figure 15 (*a*), the *y*-coordinate of *Q* is 18, and *OQ* makes an angle of 64·1° with the *y* = 0 axis. To find the length of *OQ*, look up 64·1° in the sine tables and so obtain the information in Figure 15 (*b*).

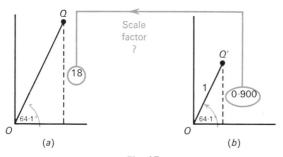

(*a*)   (*b*)

Fig. 15

What scale factor would convert 0·900 into 18? Hence find the length of *OQ*.

Exercise E

1 Find the lengths shown by question marks in Figure 16.

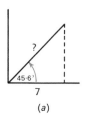
(a)

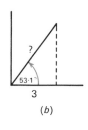
(b)

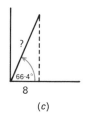
(c)

Fig. 16

2 Find the unknown lengths in Figure 17.

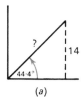
(a)

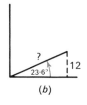
(b)

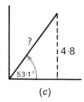
(c)

Fig. 17

3 A ladder leans against a wall at an angle of 60° to the horizontal. Its base is 3·5 m from the wall. Find the length of the ladder.

4 The jib of a crane slopes at an angle of 30° to the horizontal. The top of the jib is 22 m above the ground. What is the length of the jib assuming that the bottom is at ground level?

5 An escalator slopes at an angle of 36·9° to the horizontal. The distance between the two floors is 6 m. Find the length of the escalator.

6 A ship has sailed from port on a bearing of 053·1°. Its distance east of port is 64 km. Find the distance the ship has travelled from port.

Interlude

NINE MEN'S MORRIS

This is a game for two players.

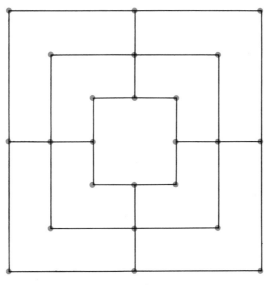

Fig. 1

Mark out a 'board' as above and obtain 18 counters—9 each, of two different colours. Take one set of counters, or 'men', per player.

Enter the men alternately, one at a time, on any vacant point. Each time a player forms a row or a 'mill' of three men along *any* line, he can remove one of his opponent's pieces, except those already in a mill.

When all the men have been entered, continue to take turns by moving a man to an adjacent vacant point along a line, trying to create more mills, thus reducing the number of your opponents pieces. A player wins by either blocking all his opponent's men so that they cannot move, or by reducing him to two pieces.

Games of this type are of very ancient origin, and are very widespread. A 'board' has been found from an Egyptian temple, dated about 1400 B.C. They were popular in Europe during the Middle Ages, and are known to have been played in Scandinavia and China.

Nine Men's Morris was played in England in Shakespeare's time, when the 'board' was cut out in turf and wooden pegs or stones were used as counters. After very wet weather, the 'board' often became unusable. In *A Midsummer Night's Dream*, Titania says: 'The nine men's morris is fill'd up with mud'.

A version of the game is still played today. The shepherd boys in Lesotho mark a board in the sand and play with stones and beans, but this is being frowned upon because it distracts them from their work! The Lesotho version is known as Marabaraba, and is played with 12 pieces each.

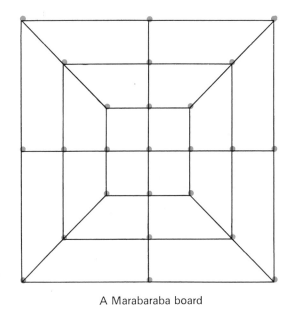

A Marabaraba board

Fig. 2

Other simpler, and early forms of the game can be played on the boards shown in Figure 3.

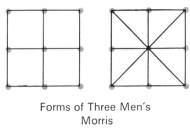

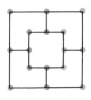

Forms of Three Men's   Six Men's Morris
Morris

Fig. 3

Whichever form of the game you decide to play, there are certain questions you should ask yourself:

(*a*) Is there an advantage in having a first turn?

(*b*) Which are the best points to occupy first?

There is a very powerful winning strategy in this form of game. Try to find it.

Revision exercises

Computation 1

1. $97 \cdot 3 + 24 \cdot 1$.

2. $101 - 93 \cdot 5$.

3. $7 \cdot 4 \times 2 \cdot 5$.

4. $1265 \div 55$.

5. $2\frac{1}{2} \times 1\frac{1}{2}$.

6. $(0 \cdot 2)^3$.

Computation 2

1. $28 \cdot 4 + 2 \cdot 84 + 0 \cdot 284$.

2. $68 \cdot 5 \times 4 \cdot 5$.

3. $7 \cdot 848 \div 36$.

4. $2\frac{2}{3} + 3\frac{1}{4} - 1\frac{5}{6}$.

5. $\dfrac{3 \cdot 6}{0 \cdot 12}$.

6. $\begin{pmatrix} -1 & 0 \\ 2 & 3 \end{pmatrix} \begin{pmatrix} 1 & 1 \\ 0 & -2 \end{pmatrix}$.

Exercise A

1. Write 81_{ten} in base eight.

2. Find the value of $a(a+b) - b(a+b)$ when $a = 5$ and $b = 3$.

3. Three men invest £30000 in the ratio 5 to 3 to 2. Find the smallest investment.

4. Write the following terminating decimals as fractions in their simplest form:
   (a) $0 \cdot 9$;   (b) $0 \cdot 84$;   (c) $7 \cdot 6$.

5. Find the values of x and y in the sequence 1, 3, 6, 10, x, 21, 28, y, ... What name is given to this sequence of numbers?

6. Onto what point is (3, 1) mapped by a reflection in $y = 0$ followed by a reflection in $x = 0$?

7. Calculate the value of x in Figure 1.

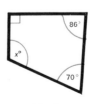

Fig. 1

8 The lengths of the two shortest sides of a right-angled triangle are 7 cm and 24 cm. Sketch the triangle and use Pythagoras's rule to find the length of the third and longest side.

Exercise B

1 Write the following numbers correct to 3 significant figures:
   (a) 111·6;   (b) 209·34;   (c) 90·08.

2 In which of the following figures are the diagonals equal in length?
   (a) Rectangle;   (b) square;
   (c) parallelogram;   (d) rhombus.

3 What must be added to $(7 + 0·7 + 0·07 + 0·007)$ to make 8?

4 What single positive rotation is equivalent to a rotation through $^+200^{\prime}$ about O followed by a rotation of $^-87°$ about O?

5 Write down the one-stage route matrix for the network in Figure 2.

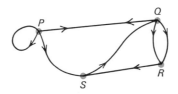

Fig. 2

6 How many planes of symmetry has a square-based pyramid?

7 An unbiased tetrahedral die is numbered from 5 to 8. What is the probability of throwing a prime number?

8 Calculate the lengths of the sides marked a, b and c in Figure 3.

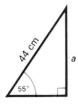 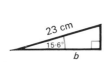

Fig. 3

Exercise C (Multi-choice)

In this exercise there may be more than one correct answer to a question. Write down the letter (or letters) corresponding to the correct answer (or answers). Show any rough working that you do.

1   The matrix product $\begin{pmatrix} 1 & 0 \\ 0 & 1 \end{pmatrix} \begin{pmatrix} 0 & ^{-}1 \\ 1 & 0 \end{pmatrix}$ is:

(a) $\begin{pmatrix} 0 & 1 \\ 1 & 0 \end{pmatrix}$;

(b) $\begin{pmatrix} 0 & ^{-}1 \\ 1 & 0 \end{pmatrix}$;

(c) $\begin{pmatrix} 0 & 1 \\ ^{-}1 & 0 \end{pmatrix}$;

(d)   none of these.

2   The value of $\sqrt{6400}$ is:
   (a)   800;   (b)   80;
   (c)   250;   (d)   none of these.

3   Which of these points lies on the line $2y = 3x - 1$?
   (a) $(1, 1)$;   (b) $(^{-}3, 4)$;
   (c) $(^{-}3, 5)$;   (d)   none of these.

4   Which of the diagrams in Figure 4 are nets for a tetrahedron?

  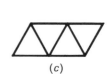

(a)   (b)   (c)   (d)

Fig. 4

5   A triangle with vertices at $(^{-}2, 2)$, $(2, 2)$, $(0, 0)$ is:
   (a)   right-angled;   (b)   equilateral;
   (c)   isosceles;   (d)   none of these.

6   34_{five} is equivalent to:
   (a) 19_{ten};   (b) 22_{six};   (c) 25_{seven};   (d) 16_{twelve}.

Exercise D

1 (*a*) Write down the one-stage route matrix for the network in Figure 5.

(*b*) Multiply this matrix by itself to give the two-stage matrix.

(*c*) How many two-stage routes are there from $Q \to P$? List them.

(*d*) Repeat (*c*) for the two-stage routes from $Q \to Q$, $Q \to R$ and $Q \to S$.

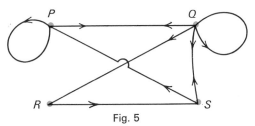

Fig. 5

2 Convert the following fractions to decimals:
$$\frac{2}{2}, \frac{2}{3}, \frac{2}{4}, \frac{2}{5}, \frac{2}{6}, \frac{2}{7}, \frac{2}{8}, \frac{2}{9}, \frac{2}{10}.$$
Compare them with your answers to Question 2 of Exercise A, Chapter 2. What do you notice?

3 The quadrilateral Q in Figure 6 is mapped onto quadrilateral Q_1 by an anticlockwise rotation of $90°$ about the origin, followed by an enlargement.

(*a*) Copy Figure 6 and show the position of Q after it has been rotated.

(*b*) Now find the centre and scale factor of the enlargement.

(*c*) The combined transformation maps A onto A_1, B onto B_1, C onto C_1 and D onto D_1. Letter the coordinates of the vertices of Q_1.

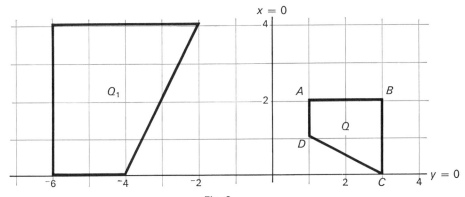

Fig. 6

51

4 A bench in a gymnasium is 3 m long and one end is raised 1 m above the ground (see Figure 7). Find the angle of slope of the bench.
   The angle of slope is increased to 35°. If you were at the top of the bench, how far would you have to jump to reach the ground?

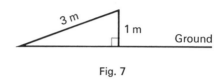

Fig. 7

5 Calculate the areas of the shapes in Figure 8 by splitting them into triangles and rectangles as shown by the dotted lines.

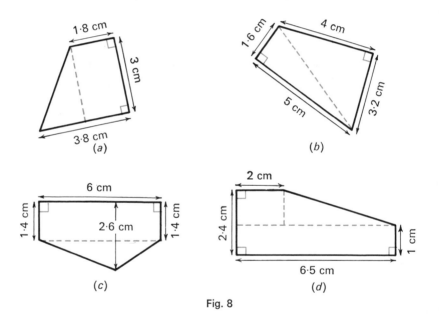

Fig. 8

6 A man leaves £12000 in his will. He leaves one-third of this to his widow. The remainder is to be shared among his three sons in the ratio of their ages which are 29, 27 and 24 years. How much do the mother and each son receive?

Exercise E

1 (*a*) Write down the one-stage route matrix for the undirected network in Figure 9.

(*b*) Work out the two-stage matrix for this network.

(*c*) The two-stage matrix should be symmetric about the leading diagonal. Why?

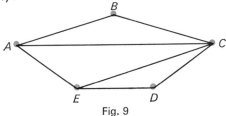

Fig. 9

2 Construct a flow diagram to give the mean of 10, 11, 12, 13, 14, 15, 16.

3 (*a*) Copy Figure 10 onto squared paper. Reflect the triangle in the line $x = 0$.

(*b*) Reflect the image in the line $y = {}^-x$.

(*c*) What single transformation would map the triangle back to its original position?

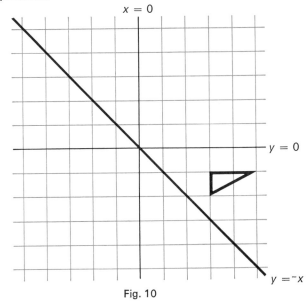

Fig. 10

(*d*) On another copy of Figure 10 reflect the triangle first in the line $y = {}^-x$ and then in the line $x = 0$. What single transformation would map the triangle back to its original position this time?

53

4   An aircraft carrier sails 420 km on a bearing of 083·5° and then alters course and sails for a further 360 km on a bearing of 046·5°. Make a sketch of the ship's journey.

   The ship's navigator wanted to end up 295 km north of the starting position. Calculate the total distance the ship went in a northerly direction and see whether he managed to do this.

   Calculate also the total distance travelled in an easterly direction.

5   $x * y$ means add x and y together and divide the result by 4. For example, $8 * 12 = 20 \div 4 = 5$.

   (*a*)   Find the value of $13 * 17$.

   (*b*)   Find the value of $2 * (3 * 5)$.

   (*c*)   Find the value of a if $a * 14 = 10$.

6   The table below shows the heights of a moving target taken at regular intervals.

Time in seconds	0	$\frac{1}{2}$	1	$1\frac{1}{2}$	2	$2\frac{1}{2}$	3	$3\frac{1}{2}$	4
Height in metres	0	9	15	19	20	19	15	9	0

Draw a graph illustrating these results with time along the axis across the page and height along the axis up the page. From your graph, answer the following questions.

(*a*)   The marksman hit the target $1\frac{3}{4}$ seconds after release. At what height was the target?

(*b*)   The marksman prefers to hit the target when it is 17 m above the ground. At what times after release can he hit the target at this height?

(*c*)   The marksman can only fire at the target when it is 10 m or more above the ground. For what length of time can he fire at the target?

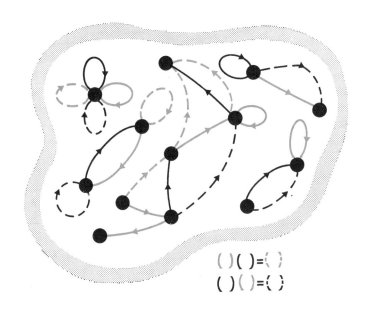

$$(\ )(\ ) = \{ \ \}$$
$$(\ )(\ ) = \{ \ \}$$

5. Matrices at work: relations

(a) Figure 1 (b) shows the relation 'is a parent of' on the set of four members of a family $\{d, e, f, g\}$.

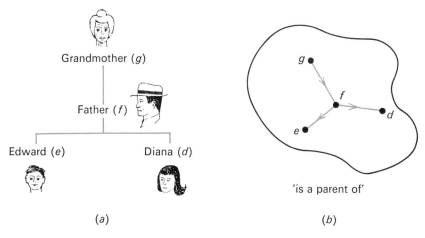

Grandmother (g)

Father (f)

Edward (e)   Diana (d)

(a)

'is a parent of'

(b)

Fig. 1

We can represent this relation by means of a matrix:

$$
\begin{array}{c}
 & \begin{array}{cccc} d & e & f & g \end{array} \\
\begin{array}{c} d \\ e \\ f \\ g \end{array} &
\left(\begin{array}{cccc}
 & & & 0 \\
0 & 0 & 0 & 0 \\
 & & & 0 \\
0 & 0 & 1 & 0
\end{array}\right).
\end{array}
$$

The 1 in the fourth row shows that *g* is a parent of *f*. The 0 in the first row shows that *d* is not a parent of *g*. Copy and complete the matrix. Call it **P**.

Is **P** symmetrical about the leading diagonal? Give a reason for your answer.

Multiply **P** by itself, that is, find the matrix P^2. Draw a diagram like the one in Figure 1 (*b*) to illustrate P^2. What relation does P^2 represent? What is the connection between this and two-stage routes?

What relation do you think P^3 would represent? Find P^3 and explain why all the numbers in the matrix are zeros.

P is the matrix which represents the relation 'is a parent of'. Try to draw a family tree for four members of a different family so that the numbers in P^3 are not all zeros.

(*b*) Copy and complete the diagram in Figure 2 (*b*) to show the relation 'is a child of' on the set {*d, e, f, g*}. What is the difference between this diagram and the one in Figure 1 (*b*)?

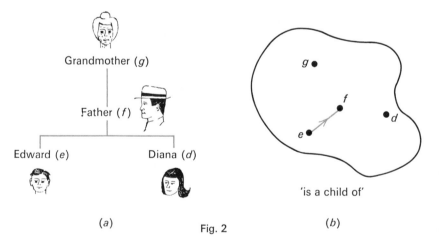

Grandmother (*g*)

Father (*f*)

Edward (*e*)   Diana (*d*)

'is a child of'

(*a*)   Fig. 2   (*b*)

Write down the matrix which represents the relation 'is a child of'. Call it **C**.

The first row of **P** is 0   0   0   0. What is the first column of **C**? The third row of **P** is 1   1   0   0. What is the third column of **C**? How can you use **P** to help you to write down **C**?

The matrix **C** can be formed from **P** by interchanging the rows and columns, that is, the first row of **P** becomes the first column of **C** and so on. The matrix **C** is called the *transpose* of **P**.

What is the transpose of **C**?

When will a matrix and its transpose be the same?

(*c*) Figure 3 shows the relation 'is a cousin of' on the set of children {*p, q, r, s, t, u, v*}. Write down

(i) the matrix which represents this relation (call it **C**);

(ii) the transpose of **C**.

What do you notice? Why does this happen?

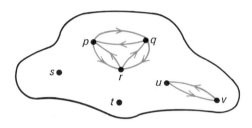

'is a cousin of'

Fig. 3

Exercise A

1 Figure 4 shows the relation 'is a brother of' on a set of four children.

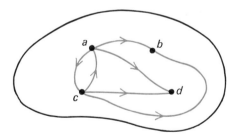

'is a brother of'

Fig. 4

(*a*) Write down the matrix which describes this relation. Call it **B**.

(*b*) Which members of the set are boys?

(*c*) Write down the transpose of **B**. What relation does it represent?

(*d*) Draw a diagram to show the relation 'is a sister of' on the same set and write down the matrix which describes this relation. Call it **S**.

2 Figure 5 shows the relation 'is a son of' on a set of five people.

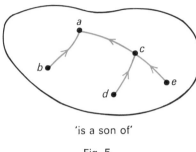

'is a son of'

Fig. 5

(*a*) Write down the matrix which describes this relation. Call it **S**.

(*b*) Find **S**^{2}. Draw a diagram to illustrate the relation which **S**^{2} represents. What is this relation?

(*c*) Can you say how many members of the set are male?

(*d*) Write down the transpose of **S**. What relation does this matrix represent?

3 (*a*) Copy and complete the diagram in Figure 6 to show the relation 'is 1 more than' on the set of numbers {0, 1, 2, 3, 4}. Write down the matrix which describes this relation. Call it **M**.

(*b*) Write down the transpose of **M**. What relation does it represent?

(*c*) Find **M**^{2}. What relation does it represent?

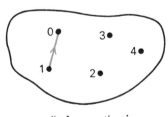

'is 1 more than'

Fig. 6

4   Figure 7 shows the relation 'is on the left of' for three people sitting round a table.

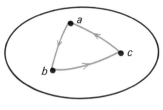

'is on the left of'

Fig. 7

(a) Write down a matrix which represents this relation. Call it **L**.

(b) What relation does the transpose of **L** represent?

(c) Find L^2. What relation does it represent? What can you say about L^2 and the transpose of **L**?

(d) Find L^3 and comment on your result.

5   Alfred, Barbara, Charles and Diana are sitting round a square table as shown in Figure 8 (a).

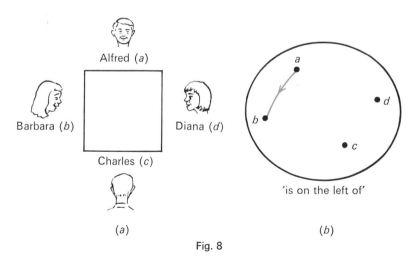

Alfred (a)

Barbara (b)   Diana (d)

Charles (c)

'is on the left of'

(a)   (b)

Fig. 8

(a) Copy and complete the diagram in Figure 8 (b) to show the relation 'is on the left of'.

(b) Write down the matrix which describes this relation. Call it **L**.

(c) Find L^2, L^3, L^4 and L^5. What relation does each of these represent? What relation would L^{29} represent?

6 (*a*) Copy and complete the diagram in Figure 9 to show the relation 'is a factor of' on the set {2, 3, 6, 7, 12}.

   (*b*) Write down the matrix which describes this relation. Call it **F**.

   (*c*) What relation does the transpose of **F** represent?

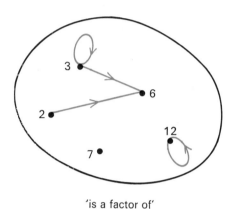

'is a factor of'

Fig. 9

7 If a matrix **T** represents the relation 'is twice' on a set of numbers, what relation is represented by (*a*) the transpose of **T**; (*b*) T^2; (*c*) T^3?

8 If a matrix **S** represents the relation 'is the square of' on a set of numbers, what relation is represented by (*a*) S^2; (*b*) the transpose of **S**?

9 Figure 10 (*a*) shows the relation 'is the daughter of' on a set of five people and Figure 10 (*b*) shows the relation 'is the sister of' on the same set.

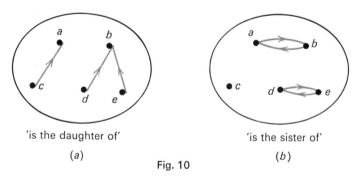

'is the daughter of'   'is the sister of'

(*a*)   (*b*)

Fig. 10

(*a*) What do the members of the set have in common?

(*b*) Write down a matrix which represents the relation shown in Figure 10 (*a*). Call it **D**.

(c) Write down a matrix which represents the relation shown in Figure 10 (b). Call it **S**.

(d) Find the matrix product **DS**. What relation does it represent?

(e) Use Figure 10 to help you to draw a diagram to show the relation 'is the sister of the mother of'.

Which matrices describe:

(i) 'is the sister of';
(ii) 'is the mother of'?

Which matrix product describes 'is the sister of the mother of'?

10 The red arrows in Figure 11 (a) represent the relation 'is the image after reflection in $y = 0$ of' and the black arrows represent the relation 'is the image after reflection in $x = 0$ of' on the set of four points $\{A, B, C, D\}$. A is the point (2, 1).

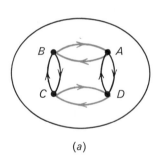

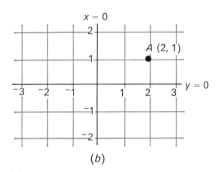

(a)   (b)

Fig. 11

(a) Copy Figure 11 (b) onto squared paper and mark the points B, C, D, giving their coordinates.

(b) Write down a matrix to describe the relation shown in red in Figure 11 (a). Call it **Y**. Now write down a matrix to describe the relation shown in black and call it **X**.

(c) Work out **XY** and **YX**, and explain why they are the same. What relation does **XY** represent?

11 (a) Draw a diagram to show the relation 'is a prime factor of' on the set $\{2, 3, 4, 5, 6\}$.

(b) Write down the matrix which represents this relation. Call it **P**.

(c) Find **P**^{2} and the transpose of **P**. What relations do these matrices represent?

12   $a \otimes b$ means multiply a by b and write down the units digit. So, for example, we write $3 \otimes 7 = 1$ or 3 multiplied by 7 gives 1. Copy and complete the following table:

		Second number			
$\otimes$		1	3	7	9
First number	1				
	3			1	
	7				
	9				

Draw separate diagrams to show each of the relations 'multiplied by 3 gives', 'multiplied by 7 gives' and 'multiplied by 9 gives' on the set $\{1, 3, 7, 9\}$. Write down matrices which describe these relations and call them **T**, **S** and **N**, respectively.

Work out **NT** and **TN** and check that both are equal to **S**. Explain carefully why this is so.

Check that **SN** = **T** and explain why this is so.

Find **N²** and explain your result.

13   Figure 12 shows three islands and the shipping routes between the ports on the islands. Copy and complete the matrix **R** to show the routes from Amber Island to Bay Island and the matrix **S** to show the routes from Bay Island to Coral Island.

$$\mathbf{R} = \begin{matrix} & b_1 \; b_2 \\ a_1 \\ a_2 \end{matrix} \begin{pmatrix} 1 & \\ & \end{pmatrix}; \qquad \mathbf{S} = \begin{matrix} & c_1 \; c_2 \; c_3 \\ b_1 \\ b_2 \end{matrix} \begin{pmatrix} & & 1 \\ & 0 & \end{pmatrix}.$$

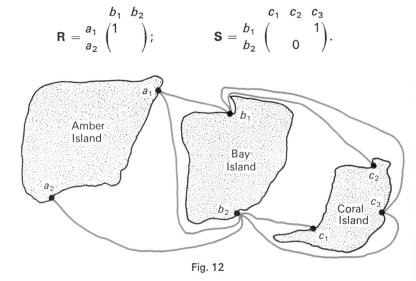

Fig. 12

(*a*) Work out **RS** and explain the meaning, if any, of your answer.

(*b*) How many different routes are there
 (i) from Amber Island to Bay Island;
 (ii) from Bay Island to Coral Island;
 (iii) from Amber Island to Coral Island calling at Bay Island on the way?

(*c*) Can you give a meaning to **SR**? (Do not look for a complicated answer.)

(*d*) Multiply the transpose of **S** by the transpose of **R** on the right. Explain the meaning of the resulting matrix.

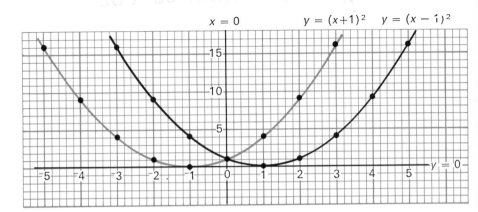

$x = 0$ $y = (x+1)^2$ $y = (x-1)^2$

6. Formulas

1. FORMULAS

1.1 Substitution in formulas

In the chapter on circles in *Book E*, we found that we could get an approximate value for the circumference of a circle by multiplying the diameter by 3. To save time this can be written as a *formula*

$$C = 3d.$$

To find the area of a circle you multiplied the radius by itself and then multiplied by 3. Write this as a formula.

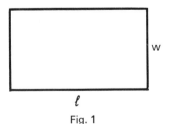

Fig. 1

The formula for finding the perimeter of a rectangle (see Figure 1) is

$$p = 2\ell + 2w.$$

Write down a formula for the area of a rectangle.

64

If we had a rectangle with $\ell = 4$ cm and $w = 3$ cm, we could find its perimeter by substituting these special values into the formula:

$$p = (2 \times 4) + (2 \times 3) \text{ cm}$$

$$= 8 + 6 \text{ cm}$$

$$= 14 \text{ cm.}$$

What would the area of the rectangle be?

Exercise A

1 If $C = 3d$, what is C when $d = 5$ cm?

2 If $p = 2\ell + 2w$, what is p when $\ell = 5\frac{1}{2}$ cm and $w = 3$ cm?

3 If $y = x^2$, what is y when $x = 4$?

4 If $D = 3a + 2b$, what is D when $a = 3$ and $b = 2\frac{1}{2}$?

5 $S = 1 \cdot 5d$. What is S when $d = 7$?

6 $A = \frac{1}{2}b + \frac{1}{3}c$. What is A when $b = 8$ and $c = 9$?

7 $y = 3x + 1$. Find y when $x = {}^-2$.

8 $z = 11x$. Find z when $x = 2 \cdot 6$.

1.2   Squaring

When you substitute values into a formula you must be careful to work out the numbers in the correct order.

For example, if you had the formula $A = 3r^2$ and were told that $r = 4$, you might think there were two possible meanings.

(*a*) First square 4 and then multiply by 3. What value does this give you?

(*b*) First multiply 4 by 3 and then square the answer. What value does this give you?

What two values might you give if $r = 2$?

It would obviously be confusing if a formula had two different meanings, so we have to decide which meaning is correct.

The formula $A = 3r^2$ means: 'To find A, first square r and then multiply by 3'. The flow diagram for this is:

$$r \longrightarrow \boxed{\text{Square}} \longrightarrow \boxed{\text{Multiply by 3}} \longrightarrow A$$

If we wanted to say: 'To find A, first multiply r by 3 and then square the answer', we would write

$$A = (3r)^2.$$

This time the flow diagram is:

$$r \longrightarrow \boxed{\text{Multiply by 3}} \longrightarrow \boxed{\text{Square}} \longrightarrow A$$

Exercise B

1 If $y = 2x^2$, what is y when $x = 3$? (Remember you first square x and then multiply by 2.)

2 If $y = (2x)^2$, what is y when $x = 3$? (Remember you first multiply x by 2 and then square the answer.)

3 $D = 3b^2$.   (a) What is D when $b = 4$?
    (b) What is D when $b = 2$?

4 $D = (3b)^2$.   (a) What is D when $b = 4$?
    (b) What is D when $b = 2$?

5 $A = (\frac{1}{2}v)^2$.   (a) What is A when $v = 2$?
    (b) What is A when $v = 6$?

6 $A = \frac{1}{2}v^2$.   (a) What is A when $v = 2$?
    (b) What is A when $v = 6$?

1.3 Punctuation

The main rule to help you remember which numbers to work out first is:
'If part of the formula is inside a bracket, work that part out first'. So
$S = 2(a+b)$ means:

'To find S, first add a and b together and then multiply by 2'.

$$a \longrightarrow \boxed{\text{Add } b} \longrightarrow \boxed{\text{Multiply by 2}} \longrightarrow S$$

Where there is no bracket the method is not so obvious. You may have forgotten the earlier work you did on this, so here are a few reminders.

(a) $C = 3a + b$ means: 'To find C, first multiply a by 3 and then add b'.

$$a \longrightarrow \boxed{\text{Multiply by 3}} \longrightarrow \boxed{\text{Add } b} \longrightarrow C$$

What is C if $a = 4$ and $b = 2$?

(b) $C = \dfrac{a+b}{3}$ means: 'To find C, first add a and b together and then divide by 3'.

$$a \longrightarrow \boxed{\text{Add } b} \longrightarrow \boxed{\text{Divide by 3}} \longrightarrow C$$

What is C if $a = 4$ and $b = 14$?

(c) Describe in your own words how to find C if $C = \dfrac{a}{3} + b$, or draw a flow diagram showing what to do.

Now find C if $a = 6$ and $b = 3$.

Exercise C

1   $A = a^2 + b^2$.   Find A if $a = 2, b = 7$.

2   $A = (a+b)^2$.   Find A if $a = 2, b = 4$.

3   $A = b^2 + c^2$.   Find A if $b = 2, c = {}^-3$.

4   $A = b^2 + c^2$.   Find A if $b = {}^-2, c = {}^-3$.

5   $A = (b+c)^2$.   Find A if $b = 4, c = {}^-2$.

6   $A = (b+c)^2$.   Find A if $b = 2, c = {}^-4$.

7   $A = (b+c)^2$.   Find A if $b = {}^-3, c = {}^-2$.

8   $y = (x-1)^2$.   Find y if $x = 12$.

9   $y = x^2 - 1$.   Find y if $x = 12$.

10   $z = (y+3)^2$.   Find z if $y = {}^-5$.

11 $y = x^2 - 5$.   Find y if $x = {}^-4$.

12 $D = 3x + 2y$.   Find D if $x = 1·5$, $y = 3·2$.

13 $X = \frac{1}{2}(Y + Z)$.   Find X if $Y = 11$, $Z = 22$.

14 $A = \dfrac{b + c}{3}$.   Find A if $b = 7$, $c = 11$.

15 $A = \dfrac{b}{3} + c$.   Find A if $b = 9$, $c = 4$.

16 $x = 2y + z$.   Find x if $y = {}^-3$, $z = 2$.

17 $F = 3g - h$.   Find F if $g = {}^-4$, $h = 2$.

18 $A = 4(a + b)$.   Find A if $a = 4$, $b = {}^-2$.

19 $X = \dfrac{c + d}{4}$.   Find X if $c = 7$, $d = {}^-2$.

20 $X = \dfrac{c}{4} + d$.   Find X if $c = 6$, $d = 3$.

2. GRAPHS

To find an approximate value for the area of a circle we use the formula

$$A = 3r^2.$$

It might be useful to make a table to give the areas of circles of different radii.

Copy and complete this table:

r (cm)	0	0·5	1	1·5	2
A (cm^2)	0	0·75			

We could continue this table to give the areas of larger circles or we could find the areas of intermediate circles, with radius less than 2 cm. In the latter case, however, it would be quicker to draw a graph to show the relation between A and r.

Draw your own graph of this relation (see Figure 2). Notice that A must be marked out up to 12 but r only goes up to 2, so you should use different scales on the two axes. Choose your scales carefully. Remember to join the points by a smooth curve.

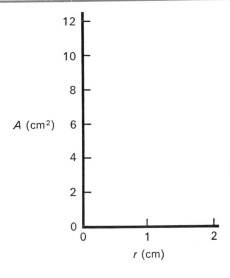

Fig. 2

From *your* graph find the approximate areas of circles with the following radii:

(*a*) *r* = 1·6 cm;   (*b*) *r* = 0·8 cm;   (*c*) *r* = 1·3 cm;   (*d*) *r* = 0·4 cm.

Exercise D

1   Copy and complete this table of values for $y = \frac{1}{2}x^2$:

x	0	1	2	3	4
y					

Use these values to draw a graph of the relation. Your axes should look like those in Figure 3. Choose your scales carefully.

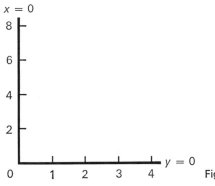

Fig. 3

2   Copy and complete this table for $y = \frac{1}{2}x^2$:

x	⁻4	⁻3	⁻2	⁻1	0	1	2	3	4
y									

Use these values to draw a graph of the relation. The axes should look like this:

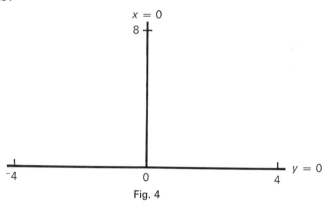

Fig. 4

3   Make a table of values for $y = (\frac{1}{2}x)^2$ with values of x between ⁻6 and 6. Draw this graph, again choosing your scales carefully. Answer the following questions from your graph:

(a) What is y when $x = 1\cdot5$?

(b) What is y when $x = 4\cdot8$?

(c) What is x when $y = 1$? (2 possible answers.)

(d) What is x when $y = 7$? (2 possible answers.)

2.1   Using graphs to solve equations

Your answers for Question 3 (c) give the solutions of the equation $(\frac{1}{2}x)^2 = 1$. Can you see why?

Check that your answers really do fit the equation.

Your answers for Question 3 (d) should give the solutions for the equation $(\frac{1}{2}x)^2 = 7$. Do your answers fit the equation exactly? If not, how do you think you could find exact solutions?

Could you solve the equation using a flow diagram?

Exercise E

1 Make a table of values for $y = x^2 - 4$ for values of x between $^-3$ and 3 and draw the graph. (You will find values of y will be between $^-4$ and 5.) Use your graph to find the solutions of:

(a) $x^2 - 4 = 4$;   (b) $x^2 - 4 = ^-2$.

Check your answers.

2 Make a table of values for $y = 2x^2$ for values of x between $^-3$ and 3 and draw the graph. From your graph find the solutions of:

(a) $2x^2 = 10$;   (b) $2x^2 = 5$.

Check your answers.

3 Make a table of values for $y = (x + 1)^2$ for values of x from $^-4$ to 2 and draw the graph. From your graph find the solutions of:

(a) $(x + 1)^2 = 7$;   (x) $(x + 1)^2 = 1 \cdot 5$.

Check your answers.

4 Make a table of values for $y = (x - 2)^2$ for values of x between $^-2$ and 6 and draw the graph. From your graph find:

(a) the value of y when $x = 1 \cdot 3$;

(b) the value of x when $y = 12 \cdot 6$;

(c) the solutions of $(x - 2)^2 = 7$.

5 Make a table of values for $y = x^2 + x - 3$ for values of x between 0 and 3 and draw the graph. Find the solutions of:

(a) $x^2 + x - 3 = 2$;   (b) $x^2 + x - 3 = ^-2$.

6 Make a table of values for $y = x^2 + x - 3$ this time for values of x between $^-4$ and 3 and draw the graph. Find the solutions of:

(a) $x^2 + x - 3 = 2$;   (b) $x^2 + x - 3 = ^-2$.

7 Make a table for $y = x^2 - x - 2$ for values of x between $^-3$ and 4. (Be very careful with the negative values of x.) Draw the graph and from it answer the following questions:

(a) What is y when $x = ^-1 \cdot 5$?

(b) What is x when $y = 2$?

(c) What are the solutions of $x^2 - x - 2 = 8$?

7. Statistics

In the statistics you have dealt with before, you will have come across three types of average. One of them is called the *arithmetic mean*. What are the others called? This chapter is concerned with the mean.

If a cricketer scores 17, 9 and 34 runs in 3 games, then his total score is $17 + 9 + 34$, which comes to 60.

His *mean* score is given by $60 \div 3$, which is 20.

Find the mean of the following groups of scores:

(*a*) 3, 5, 8, 11;

(*b*) 103, 105, 108, 111;

(*c*) 2, 2, 2, 3, 3, 3, 3, 3, 5, 5.

1. FREQUENCY TABLES

In (*c*) above, perhaps you said to yourself '3 twos and 5 threes and 2 fives, that is, 6 and 15 and 10, which add up to 31. There are 10 numbers. So the mean is $31 \div 10$, which is 3·1'.

In an example like this we say that the *frequency* of two is 3, and we can make a table showing the frequencies. Copy and complete this table:

Score	Frequency
2	3
3	
5	
Total	

Make an extra column for Score × Frequency and complete it:

Score	Frequency	Score × Frequency
2	3	6
3		
5		
Total		

Add up the entries in the right-hand column and in the frequency column. Divide the first total by the second total. You should get 3·1.

Exercise A

1 Find the means of:

(a) 5, 7, 3, 13;

(b) 305, 307, 303, 313;

(c) 25, 27, 23, 33.

2 Twenty schoolchildren had the following numbers of children in their families:

2, 3, 1, 2, 4, 3, 3, 6, 2, 2, 2, 4, 1, 3, 5, 3, 2, 3, 1, 2.

Use tally marks to complete a copy of the next frequency table, and hence find the mean size of family.

Size of family	Frequency	Size of family × Frequency
1		
2		
3		
4		
5		
6		
Total		

3 Find the frequency of family sizes in your class and draw up a frequency table. Calculate the mean.

4 A die was thrown fifty times with the following results:

Score	Frequency	Score × Frequency
1	5	
2	9	
3	7	
4	11	
5	8	
6	10	
Total		

Calculate the mean.

5 Throw a die a reasonable number of times, record your results in a frequency table, and calculate your mean score.

6 The next table shows the frequency of each score in the matches played in the four divisions of the Football League for a particular Saturday. Find the mean number of goals per team.

Score	Frequency
0	21
1	20
2	19
3	2
4	7
5	2
6	1
Total	72

7 Obtain some football results (English or Australian) and find the frequency of each score. Calculate the mean and compare it with the mean in Question 6.

2. GROUPED FREQUENCY TABLES

Figure 1 shows a bar chart for the results of an examination.

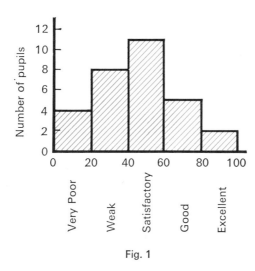

Fig. 1

Can you find the mean mark from the bar chart? If not, give a reason.

The problem is that we do not know how the marks were distributed in each grade. For example, in the 'satisfactory' grade there are 11 pupils, but we do not know whether they scored 41 or 55 or some other mark in this grade.

Can you suggest a way round this difficulty?

One method is to use the half-way value, 50, and to *estimate* that 11 pupils gained 50 marks. This would make a total of 550 marks in that grade. (But remember that this is only an estimate.)

Copy and complete this table, and use it to make an estimate of the mean:

Grade	Half-way mark m	Frequency f	$m \times f$
Very poor Weak Satisfactory Good Excellent	 50	 11	 550
	Total		

2.1 A closer look

We took the half-way mark for the 'satisfactory' grade as 50. Is that correct?

The marks in the 'excellent' grade belong to the set:

81, 82, 83, 84, 85, 86, 87, 88, 89, 90, 91, 92, 93, 94, 95, 96, 97, 98, 99, 100.

Which is the middle mark?

Check that *both* 90 *and* 91 are in the middle. Perhaps we ought to take 90·5 as the half-way mark?

What would be the half-way mark for the 'good' grade?

The marks in the 'very poor' grade belong to the set:

0, 1, 2, 3, 4, 5, 6, 7, 8, 9, 10, 11, 12, 13, 14, 15, 16, 17, 18, 19, 20.

How many numbers are there in this set? Check that the half-way mark is 10.

Here is the frequency table again with the modified half-way marks. Copy and complete the table, and use it to estimate the mean.

Grade	Half-way mark m	Frequency f	$m \times f$
Very poor	10		
Weak	30·5		
Satisfactory	50·5		
Good	70·5		
Excellent	90·5		
Total			

Check that the new estimate of the mean is not far off the first estimate.

Either method can be used, but the first method involves easier arithmetic.

2.2 The true mean

The actual marks from which the bar chart in Figure 1 was obtained are:

53, 44, 80, 22, 14, 44, 60, 47, 44, 91, 61, 8, 32, 17, 51,

62, 20, 32, 36, 47, 93, 72, 23, 34, 45, 24, 61, 57, 28, 54.

Add up these marks and divide by 30 to find the true mean.

Compare it with your estimated values. Check that the difference is not very great.

2.3 Borderline cases

From the bar chart, it is not clear whether 80, for example, counted as 'good' or 'excellent'.

It is therefore necessary to decide into which grade the borderline marks are to be put. We have put ours in the lower grade each time, so the grades really are:

0–20, 21–40, 41–60, 61–80, 81–100.

We could have put borderline marks in the upper grade and in that case the grades would be:

0–19, 20–39, 40–59, 60–79, 80–100.

It does not matter which method is used as long as it is made clear, and you stick to it.

Copy and complete the following frequency table for the examination marks given in Section 2.2. Put the borderline marks, such as 80, in the lower grade. Check that your frequencies agree with those shown in the bar chart (Figure 1). Use tally marks for recording the frequencies.

Grade	Frequency
Very poor	
Weak	
Satisfactory	
Good	
Excellent	
Total	

Exercise B

1   Using the percentage marks from a recent examination or test for your own class, draw up a frequency table with the same groups of 20 as for the bar chart in Figure 1.

Estimate the mean using half-way values. Find the true mean and compare the two.

2   The bar chart in Figure 2 shows the amount of money collected by
    60 children on a charity walk. (10p, 20p, 30p, etc., were put in the
    lower intervals.)
        Estimate the mean amount collected per child.

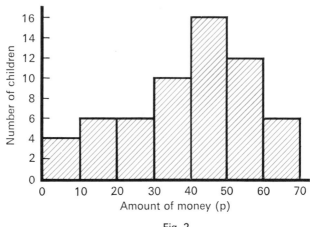

Fig. 2

3   The number of words in 100 sentences of a book were counted and
    grouped, giving the following results :

Number of words	Frequency
1–5	15
6–10	27
11–15	32
16–20	15
21–25	7
26–30	3
31–35	1
Total	100

    By using the half-way values for each group, estimate the mean
    number of words per sentence.

4   Carry out a sentence count like the one in Question 3 for a book of
    your own choice.
        Estimate the mean number of words per sentence.

3. CHOOSING GROUPS

Here again are the examination marks referred to in the previous work. This time, for ease, they are arranged in ascending order.

8, 14, 17, 20, 22, 23, 24, 28, 32, 32, 34, 36, 44, 44, 44,
45, 47, 47, 51, 53, 54, 57, 60, 61, 61, 62, 72, 80, 91, 93.

The bar chart in Figure 1 on p. 75 shows this information with the marks grouped in *twenties*.

These results could be displayed in other ways:

(*a*) You could show how many times each individual mark was obtained. The beginning of the graph would look like this:

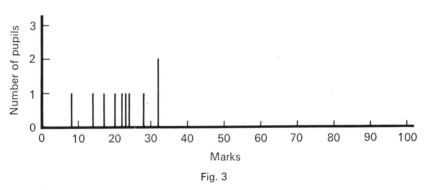

Fig. 3

Copy and complete the graph in Figure 3.

(*b*) The results could be grouped in fives: 1–5, 6–10, etc. Group the results in this way and draw a bar chart. The beginning of one is shown in Figure 4.

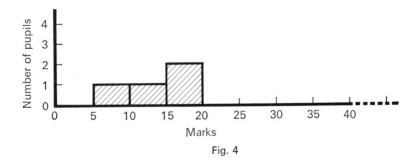

Fig. 4

(*c*) The results could be grouped in tens: 1–10, 11–20, etc. Draw a bar chart showing this.

(*d*) Draw a bar chart showing the results grouped in fifties.

(*e*) Draw a bar chart showing the results grouped in forties.

Look at all your own graphs together with the one in Figure 1 on p. 75. Which do you think presents the results most usefully? Why?

The purpose of drawing a graph is to give a clear picture of the results. Does the graph for method (*a*) give a clear picture? Can you pick out information more clearly from it than you could from just the list of results?

At the other extreme, the graph for method (*d*) only tells you how many people scored less than fifty and how many scored more than fifty. This might be useful if the pass mark was fifty and the teacher just wanted to show how many people had failed and how many had passed.

Method (*e*) does not show much detail either. There is another snag to this method. What is it?

Which grouping do you think gives the best compromise between being muddling, like (*a*), and not showing enough detail, like (*d*)?

Exercise C

1   In a small factory the weekly wages, in pounds, earned by the workers were as follows:

$$9, \quad 9, \quad 9, \quad 9, 10, 12, 12, 12, 14, 15, 15, 15,$$
$$15, 20, 20, 20, 20, 20, 25, 25, 25, 30, 35, 40.$$

(*a*) Draw up a table putting these wages in the groups 1–5, 6–10, etc.

(*b*) Draw up a table putting the wages in the groups 1–10, 11–20, etc.

(*c*) Draw up a table putting the wages in the groups 1–20, etc.

(*d*) Draw bar charts to illustrate each of your three tables.

(*e*) Which bar chart do you think shows the spread of wages most clearly?

2   (*a*) Calculate the true mean wage of the workers in Question 1.

(*b*) Calculate the approximate mean wage from the table of Question 1 (*a*).

(*c*) Do the same for the table of 1 (*b*).

(*d*) Do the same for the table of 1 (*c*).

(*e*) You now have three approximate values for the mean. Which of them is nearest to the true mean?

3   The numbers of League appearances of 24 members of a football club
(Division 3) during a season were as follows:

$$7, \quad 3, \ 28, \quad 5, \ 16, \ 45, \ 18, \quad 1,$$
$$44, \quad 2, \ 27, \quad 6, \ 43, \ 45, \quad 3, \ 34,$$
$$1, \ 34, \quad 4, \ 43, \ 45, \quad 2, \ 44, \quad 6.$$

(a) Draw up a frequency table using the groups 1–5, 6–10, etc. and
calculate the approximate mean from this table.

(b) Repeat (a) using the groups 1–10, 11–20, etc.

(c) Which of the approximate means do you think is nearer the true
mean? Calculate the true mean and see if you were right.

4   Sixty 15-year-old boys were tested to find their pulse-rate when they
were resting. The following figures were obtained for the number of
beats per minute:

72	70	66	74	81	70	74	53	57	62
58	92	74	67	62	91	73	64	65	80
78	67	75	80	83	61	72	72	69	70
76	74	65	84	79	80	76	72	68	65
82	79	71	86	77	69	72	56	70	62
76	56	86	63	73	70	75	73	89	64

(a) Put these results in the groups 51–55, 56–60, etc. and calculate
the approximate mean.

(b) Calculate the approximate mean which you obtain by putting the
results in the groups 51–60, 61–70, etc.

(c) Calculate the approximate mean which you obtain by putting the
results in the groups 51–70, etc.

(d) Finding the true mean would take a long time for this question.
Do you think your estimates for the mean are good ones? Why?

8. Lengths, areas and volumes of similar objects

1. SCALE MODELS

Figure 1 shows a drawing of a scale model of the Concorde. The model was carefully constructed so that externally it has the same shape as the actual aircraft. It was made on a scale of 1 to 100. This means that all the lengths on the model are $\frac{1}{100}$ of the corresponding lengths on the aircraft.

Fig. 1

(a) The length of the Concorde is approximately 59 m. What is the length of the model?

(*b*) The wing span of the model is 25·5 cm. What is the wing span of the aircraft?

(*c*) On the model, the angle between the leading edge of the wing and the fuselage is 25°. What is the size of the corresponding angle on the aircraft?

> When two objects have the same shape:
>   (i) All the lengths of one object are a fixed number times the corresponding lengths of the other. This number is called the scale factor.
>   (ii) Corresponding angles are equal.
> Objects which have the same shape are called *similar*.

Exercise A

1   A toy car is 3·9 cm long. It is made on a scale of 1 to 100. What is the length of the real car?

2   A model aircraft is 40 cm long. It is made on a scale of 1 to 50. What is the length of the actual aircraft?

3   A model of a new liner is made on a scale of 1 to 200. Copy and complete the following table:

	Liner	Model
Length	320 m	
Beam	35 m	
Draught	10 m	

4   A scale model of a bus is 3 cm high and the real bus is 3·6 m high. What is the scale of the model? What is the ratio of the length of the bus to the length of the model?

5   The lengths of the sides of a triangle are 6 cm, 9 cm, 12 cm. The shortest side of a similar triangle is 3 cm long. Find the lengths of the other two sides.

83

6 Accurate models of the following pieces of furniture are to be made for a doll's house. If a scale of 1 to 10 is used, what size will the doll's house furniture have to be made?

   (*a*) A television set (60 cm by 50 cm by 35 cm);

   (*b*) a bed (1·8 m by 0·8 m);

   (*c*) a piano (1·2 m by 1·25 m by 0·5 m).

7 A photograph is 10 cm long and 8 cm wide. A smaller print of the same photograph is 5 cm long. What is its width?
   What would be the length of a print which is 2 cm wide?

8 A map of a school is made using a scale of 1 to 1000. What is the size on the map of:

   (*a*) a classroom 10 m by 12 m;

   (*b*) the hall 66 m by 20 m;

   (*c*) a playing field 120 m by 100 m?

9 The scale of a map is 1 to 50000. What is the distance in kilometres represented by (*a*) 1 cm; (*b*) 5 cm on the map?

10 The scale of a map is 1 to 20000. What is the distance in kilometres represented by 8 cm on the map?

11 A triangle has angles of 40°, 50°, 90°, and the length of its longest side is 10 cm. The longest side of a similar triangle is 5 cm. What are the sizes of its angles?

12 Figure 2 shows two space capsules. Compare the lengths marked on the figure and say whether you think the capsules are similar. (Figure 2 is not drawn to scale.)

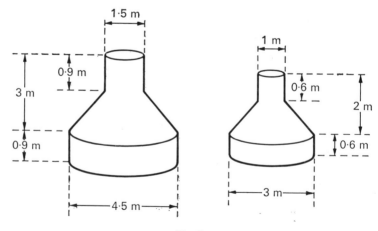

Fig. 2

13 A toy shop has two models of a popular family car in stock. The first model is 15 cm long, 7·2 cm wide and 5 cm high. The second model is 5 cm long, 2·4 cm wide and 1·5 cm high. Both models are advertised as 'accurate scale models'. Is this possible? Give a reason for your answer.

14 A photograph, which is 5 cm wide and 22 cm long, is mounted on a piece of white card so that a white border 3 cm wide shows all the way round the photograph. Find the width and length of the card. Are the shapes of the card and the photograph similar?

2. AREAS OF SIMILAR OBJECTS

Figure 3 shows a square of side 1 cm and an enlargement, scale factor 2.

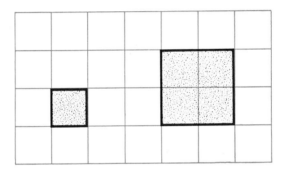

Fig. 3

How many squares identical to the smaller square can you fit into the larger one?

What is the ratio of the length of a side of the smaller square to the length of a side of the larger one?

What is the ratio of the area of the smaller square to the area of the larger one?

Investigation 1

Figure 4 shows a rectangle and an enlargement, scale factor 2.

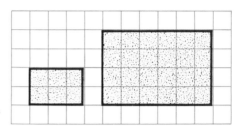

Fig. 4

On centimetre squared paper, make four copies of the smaller rectangle and one copy of the larger one and cut them out. Can you fit the four smaller rectangles into the larger one? If so, draw a diagram to show how this can be done.

What is the ratio of the area of the smaller rectangle to the area of the larger one?

Figures 5, 6 and 7 show some more enlargements with scale factor 2. In each case, cut from centimetre squared paper four copies of the smaller shape and one copy of the larger one. Can you fit the four smaller shapes into the larger one? If so, show clearly how this can be done.

Fig. 5

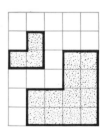

Fig. 6

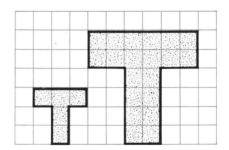

Fig. 7

Unless you cut some of the smaller T's into pieces, you would have been unable to fit the four smaller T's into the larger one. Check, by counting squares, that the area of the larger T is nevertheless four times the area of the smaller one.

If an object is enlarged with scale factor 2, what is the ratio of

(*a*) lengths on the original object to corresponding lengths on the new object;

(*b*) the area of the original object to the area of the new object?

Investigation 2

Figure 8 shows a trapezium. What is its area in cm²?

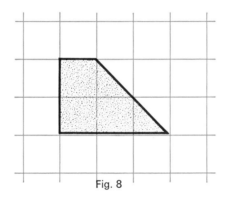

Fig. 8

Copy the trapezium onto squared paper. Choose a centre of enlargement and enlarge the trapezium with scale factor 3. Find the area of the new trapezium.

What is the ratio of

(*a*) lengths on the original trapezium to corresponding lengths on the new trapezium;

(*b*) the area of the original trapezium to the area of the new trapezium?

Repeat this work for several shapes of your own choice and comment on your results.

Investigation 3

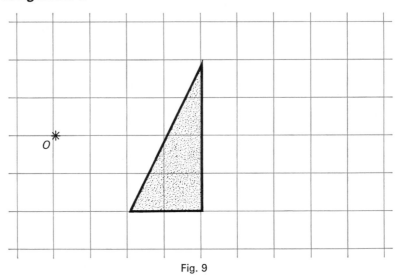

Fig. 9

Copy Figure 9 onto a large sheet of squared paper. Enlarge the triangle with centre O and scale factor $1\frac{1}{2}$.

What is the ratio of lengths on the original triangle to corresponding lengths on the new triangle?

Find the area of the original triangle and the area of the new triangle.

What is the ratio of the original area to the new area?

Repeat this work using scale factors 2, $2\frac{1}{2}$, 3, $3\frac{1}{2}$, $\frac{1}{2}$. Draw all your triangles on the same diagram and enter your results in a copy of the following table:

(a) Scale factor	(b) Ratio of original lengths to corresponding new lengths	(c) Original area	(d) New area	(e) Ratio of original area to new area
$1\frac{1}{2}$	1 to $1\frac{1}{2}$ = 2 to 3	4 cm²	9 cm²	4 to 9
2	1 to 2	4 cm²		
$2\frac{1}{2}$	1 to $2\frac{1}{2}$ =			
3	1 to 3			
$3\frac{1}{2}$	1 to $3\frac{1}{2}$ =			
$\frac{1}{2}$	1 to $\frac{1}{2}$ =			

Compare your entries in columns (b) and (e) and try to explain any connection between them.

A model of an aeroplane is made on a scale of 1 to 10. State the ratio of

(*a*) lengths on the model to corresponding lengths on the aeroplane;

(*b*) lengths on the aeroplane to corresponding lengths on the model;

(*c*) areas on the model to corresponding areas on the aeroplane;

(*d*) areas on the aeroplane to corresponding areas on the model.

Copy and complete the following table:

	Model	Aeroplane
Wing span	2·1 m	
Length of fuselage		26 m
Surface area of wings	1·84 m²	
Number of seats		60

Exercise B

1 If the lengths of the sides of a rectangle are each doubled, what happens to its area?

2 A tile 8 cm long has an area of 20 cm². Another tile of the same shape is 16 cm long. What is its area?

3 If the lengths of the sides of a rectangle are each halved, what happens to its area?

4 A label 6 cm wide has an area of 60 cm². What is the area of a similar label 3 cm wide?

5 A photograph is 20 cm long and 15 cm wide. The length of a small print of the same photograph is 5 cm. Find (*a*) the width of the smaller print; (*b*) the area of the smaller print.

6 3 kg of fertilizer are needed for a rectangular plot. How much fertilizer would be needed for a plot of double the dimensions?

7 1 kg of grass seed is needed for a rectangular plot 25 m long. How much seed would be needed for a similar plot which is 75 m long?

8 72 lino tiles, each 30 cm square, are needed in order to cover a kitchen floor. How many tiles would be needed if tiles, each 15 cm square, were used instead?

9 All circles have the same shape. One circle has four times the radius of another circle. How many times greater is its area?

10 All spheres are similar. One sphere has three times the diameter of another sphere. How many times greater is its surface area?

11 A balloon is approximately spherical. How many times does its surface area increase when it is blown up from a diameter of 5 cm to a diameter of 30 cm?

12 A model village was made on a scale of 1 to 10. Copy and complete the following table:

Object	Model village	Real village
Length of cottage		10 m
Height of cottage	0·48 m	
Floor area of cottage	0·55 m²	
Area of village green		1200 m²
Area of duck pond	4·25 m²	
Area of fire station doors		36 m²
Cost of painting doors	2p	

13 A length of 10 km is represented by 20 cm on a map.

(a) What length in km does 1 cm represent?

(b) What area in km² does 1 cm² represent?

(c) A forest is represented on the map by an area of 3 cm². What is the area of the forest?

(d) What area on the map represents a region of area 120 km²?

14 The area of a lake is 8 km² and is represented by an area of 2 cm² on a map.
What area in km² is represented by 1 cm² on the map?
What length in km is represented by 1 cm on the map?
What is the ratio of lengths on the map to actual lengths?

15 The scale of a map is 1 to 50000. A wood occupies 16 cm² on the map. How many square kilometres does the wood actually cover?

3. VOLUMES OF SIMILAR OBJECTS

Investigation 4

Figure 10 shows three cubes. Cube *A* is of side 1 cm, cube *B* is of side 3 cm and cube *C* is of side 5 cm.

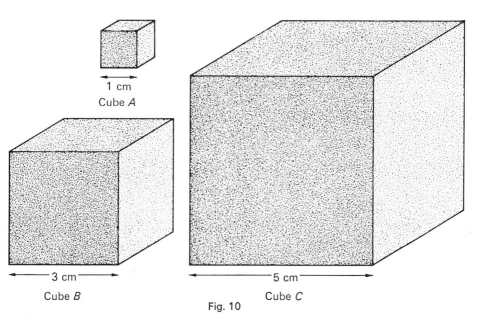

1 cm

Cube *A*

3 cm

Cube *B*

5 cm

Cube *C*

Fig. 10

(*a*) Do all cubes have the same shape?

(*b*) For each cube, calculate
   (i)   the surface area (the total area of the six faces) ;
   (ii) the volume.

(*c*) Write down the ratio of
   (i)   the height of cube *A* to the height of cube *B* ;
   (ii) the surface area of cube *A* to the surface area of cube *B* ;
   (iii) the volume of cube *A* to the volume of cube *B*.

(*d*) Write down the ratio of
   (i)   the height of cube *A* to the height of cube *C* ;
   (ii) the surface area of cube *A* to the surface area of cube *C* ;
   (iii) the volume of cube *A* to the volume of cube *C*.

(*e*) Write down the ratio of
   (i)   the height of cube *C* to the height of cube *B* ;
   (ii) the surface area of cube *C* to the surface area of cube *B* ;
   (iii) the volume of cube *C* to the volume of cube *B*.

4-2

(*f*) Write down the ratio of
(i) the height of a 2 cm cube to the height of a 6 cm cube;
(ii) the surface area of a 2 cm cube to the surface area of a 6 cm cube.

What do you think is the ratio of the volume of a 2 cm cube to the volume of a 6 cm cube? Work out the volumes of these two cubes and check whether or not you were right.

Investigation 5

You will need a large pile of identical match-boxes for this investigation.

Use 4 match-boxes to build the shape shown in Figure 11. Now use match-boxes to build an enlargement with scale factor 2, that is, make all the lengths of your new shape twice as long as the corresponding lengths of the shape shown in Figure 11. How many boxes do you need?

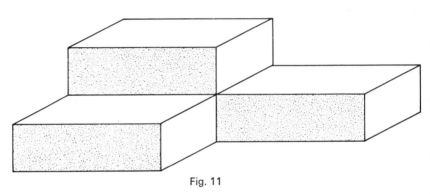

Fig. 11

How many boxes do you think you will need to make an enlargement with scale factor 3? Build this enlargement and see whether you were right.

Make some other shapes with match-boxes. Forecast how many boxes you will need in order to build enlargements with scale factors 2 and 3. Build these enlargements and check whether your forecasts were correct.

Exercise C

1 If all the lengths of a box are doubled, what happens to
(*a*) its surface area;
(*b*) its volume?

2 If the measurements of a box are each trebled, what happens to
(*a*) its surface area;
(*b*) its volume?

3   If the measurements of a box are each halved, what happens to

   (*a*) its surface area;

   (*b*) its volume?

4   A box of height 3 cm has a volume of 240 cm^3. What is the volume of a similar box of height 6 cm?

5   A toy building brick is 2 cm thick and has a volume of 80 cm^3. What would be the volume of a similar brick 1 cm thick?

6   A box 5 cm long has a volume of 30 cm^3. What is the volume of a similar box which is 15 cm long?

7   A container 8 cm high has a volume of 600 cm^3. What is the volume of a similar container 40 cm high?

8   A small packet of Sludge washing powder is 4 cm wide and contains 0·8 kg of powder. The giant size is sold in a similar packet which is 6 cm wide. How much powder does it contain?

9   A model of a house is made on a scale of 1 to 20. Write down:

   (*a*) the ratio of areas on the model to areas on the house;

   (*b*) the ratio of volumes on the model to volumes on the house.

   The house is 10 m high, has a floor area of 120 m^2 and a cubic capacity (volume) of 320 m^3. Find the height, floor area and cubic capacity of the model.

10   Two spherical balls have diameters of 4 cm and 8 cm. Find

   (*a*) the ratio of their diameters in its simplest form;

   (*b*) the ratio of their surface areas;

   (*c*) the ratio of their volumes.

11   Two solid spheres are made from the same material. One has a diameter of 10 cm and weighs 20 kg. The other has a diameter of 5 cm. How much does it weigh?

12   Two spheres have diameters of 40 cm and 30 cm. Write down in its simplest form the ratio of

   (*a*) their diameters;

   (*b*) their surface areas;

   (*c*) their volumes.

13   The two cylinders shown in Figure 12 are similar and filled with oil. The smaller one contains 3 litres of oil. How much does the larger one contain?

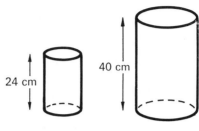

Fig. 12

14   A glass is 8 cm high and the diameter of its rim is 4 cm. The height of a larger glass of the same shape is 12 cm.

(*a*) Find the diameter of the rim of the larger glass.

(*b*) What is the ratio of the volume of the larger glass to that of the smaller glass?

15   A solid lead sphere of diameter 10 cm weighs 5 kg. How much would a solid lead sphere of diameter 12 cm weigh?

16   Two similar boxes have volumes of 200 cm³ and 1600 cm³. Write down in its simplest form the ratio of

(*a*) their volumes;

(*b*) their heights.

17   Two similar boxes have volumes of 125 cm³ and 27 cm³. What is the ratio of

(*a*) their heights;

(*b*) their surface areas?

18   Two similar jugs hold $\frac{1}{4}$ litre and 2 litres respectively. The height of the smaller jug is 15 cm. Find the height of the other one.

19   Two spheres have surface areas of 9 cm² and 4 cm². What is the ratio of

(*a*) their diameters;

(*b*) their volumes?

20   A solid bronze model of a statue is 50 cm high and weighs 30 kg. The full size statue is 4·5 m high. What would it weigh if it were made of solid bronze?

21 Two ball bearings have volumes of 1·6 cm³ and 5·4 cm³. Find

   (*a*) the ratio of their volumes in its simplest form;

   (*b*) the ratio of their diameters;

   (*c*) the ratio of their surface areas.

22 A village inn has a model of the village in its garden. The High Street
   is 480 m long and in the model it is 6 m long. What is the scale of the
   model?

   The area of the recreation ground is 0·7 m² in the model. What is its
   true area?

   In the model garden of the model inn, there is, of course, a model of
   the model of the village. How long is the High Street in this model?

23 Read 'On being the right size' by J. B. S. Haldane in *The World of
   Mathematics*, Volume 2.

Interlude

COIN SHAPES

In *Book D* we mentioned the 50p coin as being an unusual and interesting shape and we looked at some of the properties of this family of shapes.

Most other coins are circular, but what other shape of coin is there, or has there been?

Figure 1 shows three examples. See if you can find any more.

(Look through coin magazines or look in the windows of coin dealers.)

Try to find the correct mathematical names for the shapes you discover. If you cannot find one, make one up.

| The British 3d | Cyprus piastre | Greek 10 lepta |

Fig. 1

Why are most coins circular? The circular shape has certain disadvantages. It can roll away when it is dropped and is also very wasteful of metal when it is stamped from a strip:

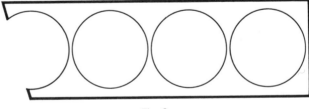

Fig. 2

Investigate the advantages and disadvantages of different coin shapes. How are coins made today? How were early coins made?

Revision exercises

Computation 3

1. $9{\cdot}9 + 0{\cdot}99$.

2. $230 - 9{\cdot}1$.

3. $48 \times 0{\cdot}45$.

4. $^{-}7(5 + {^{-}2})$.

5. $2268 \div 3{\cdot}6$.

6. $\frac{3}{4} \div \frac{7}{8}$.

Computation 4

1. $148{\cdot}7 + 39{\cdot}3 - 99{\cdot}4$.

2. $2{\cdot}6 \times 3{\cdot}5 \times 0{\cdot}5$.

3. 15% of £750.

4. $\dfrac{13{\cdot}6 \times 40}{5}$.

5. Find the value of $16 \times$ cosine of $73°$.

6. $\begin{pmatrix} 7 & ^{-}1 & 2 \\ 0 & ^{-}3 & 4 \end{pmatrix} + \begin{pmatrix} ^{-}4 & 3 & 2 \\ 1 & ^{-}3 & 0 \end{pmatrix}$.

Exercise F

1. What number comes next? 2, 5, 10, 17, 26, ?.

2. If $A = 3r^2$, what is A when $r = 11$?

3. (a) Work out: $1101_{two} + 1010_{two} + 11011_{two} + 10111_{two}$, leaving your answer in base two.

   (b) Give the answer as a decimal number.

4. Onto what point is $(^{-}1, 1)$ mapped by the translation with vector $\begin{pmatrix} ^{-}3 \\ 2 \end{pmatrix}$?

5. A 3 by 4 matrix is multiplied by a 4 by 5 matrix. What is the order of the answer?

6. The area of a rectangle is 5 cm². What is the area of an enlargement with scale factor 3?

7. In a co-educational school, three-fifths of the pupils are boys. How many pupils has the school if there are 660 boys?

8. The concrete base of a garage is 6 m by 2 m and the concrete is 18 cm thick. What is the volume of the concrete in cubic metres?

Revision exercises

Exercise G

1   Write down a fraction whose value lies between $\frac{1}{3}$ and $\frac{3}{8}$.

2   Find the mean of 81·6, 88·1, 87·9, 89·0, 85·4.

3   Give rough estimates of the answers to the following:
     (a) 8900×0.837;   (b) $26.1 \div 0.46$.

4   $C = \frac{3}{4}(a - 10)$. Find C if $a = 30$.

5   Draw a network described by the following route matrix:

$$\begin{pmatrix} 0 & 0 & 1 & 0 \\ 0 & 0 & 1 & 1 \\ 1 & 1 & 0 & 0 \\ 0 & 1 & 0 & 0 \end{pmatrix}.$$

6   Between which two whole numbers does $\sqrt{1500}$ lie?

7   Draw one letter of the alphabet which is topologically equivalent to A.

8   What number base is being used if $35 + 43 = 111$?

Exercise H (*Multi-choice*)

In this exercise there may be more than one correct answer to a question. Write down the letter (or letters) corresponding to the correct answer (or answers). Show any rough working that you do.

1   Which of the following fractions is the largest?
     (a) $\frac{3}{5}$;   (b) $\frac{1}{3}$;   (c) $\frac{1}{2}$;   (d) $\frac{3}{4}$.

2   Which of the networks in Figure 1 can be described by the matrix

$$\begin{array}{c} \\ A \\ B \\ C \end{array} \begin{array}{ccc} A & B & C \\ \begin{pmatrix} 2 & 2 & 0 \\ 2 & 2 & 1 \\ 0 & 1 & 0 \end{pmatrix} \end{array}?$$

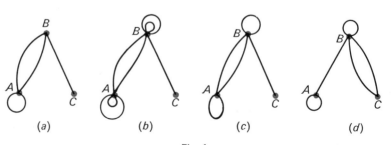

(a)   (b)   (c)   (d)

Fig. 1

3 The nearest rough estimate of $\dfrac{0{\cdot}8 \times 111}{0{\cdot}9}$ is

(*a*) 11;   (*b*) 110;   (*c*) 1100;   (*d*) 1000.

4 Which of the following transformations map the point (3, 2) onto ($^-$3, $^-$2)?

(*a*) Translation described by the vector $\begin{pmatrix} 6 \\ 4 \end{pmatrix}$;

(*b*) Rotation about (0, 0) through 180°;

(*c*) Reflection in the line $y = {}^-x$;

(*d*) Translation described by the vector $\begin{pmatrix} -6 \\ -4 \end{pmatrix}$.

5 If you draw a card at random from a full pack of 52 cards (jokers excluded), then the probability that you draw:

(i) a spade is:

(*a*) $\frac{1}{4}$;   (*b*) $\frac{1}{13}$;   (*c*) $\frac{1}{52}$;   (*d*) none of these;

(ii) a queen is:

(*a*) $\frac{1}{4}$;   (*b*) $\frac{1}{13}$;   (*c*) $\frac{1}{52}$;   (*d*) none of these.

6 Which of the following values of x satisfy the equation $x^2 = 16$?

(*a*) 4;   (*b*) 8;   (*c*) $^-$4;   (*d*) none of these.

Exercise I

1 Figure 2 (*a*) shows the relation 'is the nephew of', on a set of five people and Figure 2 (*b*) shows the relation 'is the brother of' on the same set.

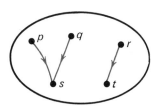
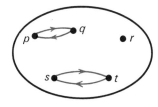

'is the nephew of'   'is the brother of'

(*a*)   Fig. 2   (*b*)

(*a*) Write down a matrix which represents the relation shown in Figure 2 (*a*). Call it **N**.

(*b*) Write down a matrix which represents the relation shown in Figure 2 (*b*). Call it **B**.

(*c*) Write down the transpose of **N** and the transpose of **B**. What do you notice?

(*d*) What relation does each of the transposes of **N** and **B** represent?

(*e*) How is *r* related to each of *p*, *q* and *s*?

2 In each of the following, find *A* given that $a = 2$, $b = {}^-2$ and $c = {}^-1$.

(*a*) $A = \jmath b + 4c$;

(*b*) $A = a^2 + b^2$;

(*c*) $A = (b + c)^2$;

(*d*) $A = b^2 - (c + a)$.

3 Fifty fourteen-year-olds were asked to guess how many peas there were in a packet of frozen peas. Their guesses were as follows:

```
399  310  420  315  506  253  489  396  418  520
417  400  328  300  590  438  403  599  423  389
327  548  422  402  498  512  311  406  507  434
411  523  355  478  347  522  507  302  329  421
590  409  377  530  600  427  450  400  391  599
```

Draw up a grouped frequency table using the groups 251–300, 301–350, 351–400, etc. Use this table to estimate the mean guess.

4 A scale model of a London Transport bus is made to a scale of $\frac{1}{10}$. The following measurements are for the actual bus. What are the corresponding measurements for the model?

(*a*) Length 30 m;

(*b*) width 2 m;

(*c*) area of upper floor 44 m²;

(*d*) capacity of fuel tank 320 litres;

(*e*) number of seats 56;

(*f*) diameter of turning circle 16 m.

5 On centimetre squared paper, draw $x = 0$ and $y = 0$ axes with values of *x* between 0 and 11 and values of *y* between 0 and 9. Plot each of the following sets of points and join them up to form quadrilaterals. Calculate the area (in cm²) of each quadrilateral.

(*a*) (0, 7), (1, 9), (4, 7), (1, 3);

(*b*) (7, 5), (5, 7), (9, 9), (11, 7);

(*c*) (4, 2), (10, 4), (8, 2), (10, 0).

6 24% of the 25 girls in a fourth year form came to school with dresses that were the wrong length. Two-thirds of this number altered them the same evening. How many girls failed to do so?

Exercise J

1   Draw a diagram to show the relation 'is a multiple of' on the set {3, 6, 9, 12}.

   (a) Represent this relation by means of a matrix. Call it **R**.

   (b) Write down the transpose of **R**.

   (c) What relation does the transpose of **R** represent?

2   Make a table of values for $y = (x-3)^2$ for values of x between $^-2$ and 8 and draw the graph. From your graph find

   (a) the value of y when $x = 2 \cdot 1$;

   (b) the value of x when $y = 4 \cdot 7$;

   (c) the solutions of $(x-3)^2 = 20$.

3   A school entered 110 candidates for the C.S.E. Mathematics examination. The following table shows their results:

Marks	Frequency
21–30	1
31–40	3
41–50	10
51–60	35
61–70	50
71–80	7
81–90	4

   Estimate the mean average mark.

   From this table, draw up a table which groups the marks 21–40, 41–60, etc. Would you expect the entries in the new table to give you a higher or lower estimate of the mean mark? Try to explain why. Then do the calculation to see whether you were right.

4   The carpets shown in Figure 3 are similar in shape and are made of the same material. The cost of the smaller carpet is £30. How much would you expect to pay for the larger one?

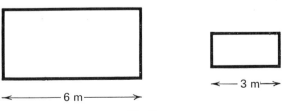

Fig. 3

5 The following triangular pattern of numbers can be continued indefinitely.

```
              1
           1     3
         1    3    5
       1    3    5    7
     1    3    5    7    9
   1    3    5    7    9    11
```

(a) What is the sum of the numbers in the sixth row?

(b) Write down the seventh row and calculate its sum.

(c) What is the sum of the numbers in the tenth row?

(d) Which row has a sum of 169?

6 Figure 4 shows just three sides of a regular polygon. How many sides does it have altogether?

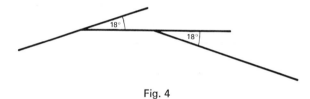

Fig. 4

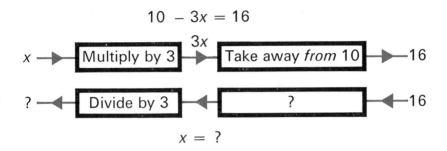

$$10 - 3x = 16$$

x → Multiply by 3 → $3x$ → Take away *from* 10 →—16

? ← Divide by 3 ← ? ←—16

$$x = ?$$

9. Solutions of equations

1. METHOD A: INVERSE OPERATIONS

1.1 Negative numbers

You will need to be able to work with negative numbers in this chapter. Work through Exercise A for revision. Make sure that you have got all the questions right before going any further.

Exercise A

1   $2 - {}^-3$.

2   ${}^-3 - {}^-2$.

3   $5 - 7$.

4   Take 8 away from 6.

5   Take ${}^-2$ away from 4.

6   Take ${}^-3$ away from ${}^-5$.

7   Take 3 away from ${}^-2$.

8   ${}^-8 \div 4$.

9   ${}^-5 \times 2$.

10   ${}^-9 \div 4$.

11   ${}^-7 + {}^-5$.

12   Add ${}^-6$ to ${}^-4$.

1.2 Flow diagrams for simple equations

Figure 1 should remind you how to solve the equation $2x + 3 = 5$ by flow diagrams.

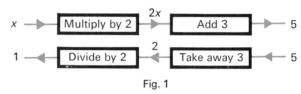

Fig. 1

So $x = 1$.

In reversing the diagram, we first take away 3 because the operation 'take away 3' is the opposite, or *inverse operation* for 'add 3'.
What is the inverse operation for 'multiply by 2'?

Exercise B

Solve the following equations, using flow diagrams.

1   $2x + 3 = 6$.   2 $2(x - 1) = 8$.

3   $3x - 5 = 7$.   4 $4(x + 2) = 14$.

5   $3(2x - 1) = {}^-9$.   6 $2(3x + 4) = 10$.

7   $3x + 4 = 1$.   8 $\frac{1}{3}(x + 3) = {}^-4$.

9   $\frac{x}{2} - 8 = 2$.   10 $x - 8 = 2$.

1.3 Equations with ' $-x$ '

Question 10 probably seemed very easy. You should have got these flow diagrams:

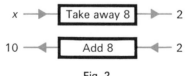

Fig. 2

So $x = 10$.

We now want to construct flow diagrams to solve $8 - x = 2$. We must start with x, and then take it away *from* 8 :

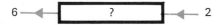

$$x \longrightarrow \boxed{\text{Take away } from \text{ 8}} \longrightarrow 2$$

How can we reverse this flow diagram? We need to know the inverse operation for 'take away *from* 8'.
Is it 'add onto 8'?
What answer would this give?
Does it fit the question?

We can spot the correct answer easily enough. It is 6, so our reverse flow diagram must look like this :

$$6 \longleftarrow \boxed{\qquad ? \qquad} \longleftarrow 2$$

What possible operations could be put in the box?

It could be 'add 4' or 'multiply by 3', but these do not seem to have much connection with the equation, $8 - x = 2$.

It could also be 'take away *from* 8'. The flow diagrams would then be as shown in Figure 3 :

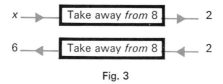

$$x \longrightarrow \boxed{\text{Take away } from \text{ 8}} \longrightarrow 2$$
$$6 \longleftarrow \boxed{\text{Take away } from \text{ 8}} \longleftarrow 2$$

Fig. 3

So $x = 6$.

It would seem that the inverse operation for 'take away *from* 8' might be 'take away *from* 8'.

1.4 Self-inverse mappings

You did some work on inverse mappings in *Book D*. We shall now consider some questions like the ones you met then.

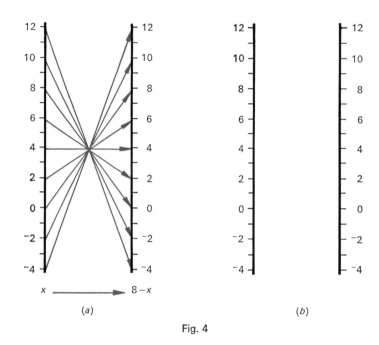

(a)   (b)

Fig. 4

Figure 4 (*a*) shows the mapping diagram for $x \to 8 - x$. Copy Figures 4 (*a*) and (*b*) and complete (*b*) to show the inverse mapping for $x \to 8 - x$. (For example, in Figure 4 (*a*), $0 \to 8$, so in Figure 4 (*b*), $8 \to 0$; in Figure 4 (*a*), $2 \to 6$, so in Figure 4 (*b*), $6 \to 2$; etc.)

What do you notice about the two diagrams?

When a mapping diagram and its inverse are exactly the same, we have a *self-inverse mapping*.

Draw the mapping diagram for $x \to 6 - x$ and its inverse. Is $x \to 6 - x$ a self-inverse mapping?

Just as mappings like $x \to 8 - x$ and $x \to 6 - x$ are *self-inverse mappings*, so operations like 'take away *from* 8', which we met in the equation $8 - x = 2$, are *self-inverse operations*.

Figure 5 shows how we can use this idea to solve

$$6 - x = 3.$$

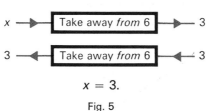

$$x = 3.$$

Fig. 5

Does this answer fit the equation?

Figure 6 shows the solution of

$$4 - x = 6.$$

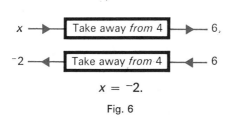

$$x = {}^-2.$$

Fig. 6

Copy and complete Figure 7 to solve

$$2 - x = {}^-5.$$

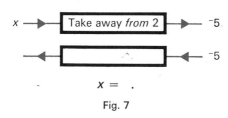

$$x = .$$

Fig. 7

Does your answer fit the equation?

Exercise C

Solve the following equations. Even if you can spot the answer, draw the flow diagrams, so that you get used to the method.

1 $7 - x = 2.$ 2 $4 - x = {}^-3.$

3 $3 - x = 5.$ 4 $2 - x = {}^-4.$

5 $13 - x = {}^-2.$	6 ${}^-2 - x = 4.$
7 ${}^-3 - x = 2.$	8 ${}^-4 - x = {}^-3.$
9 $4 = 6 - x.$	10 $5 = 3 - x.$

1.5   Equations with '$-2x$', '$-3x$', etc.

Figure 8 shows the flow diagrams to solve

$$10 - 2x = 4.$$

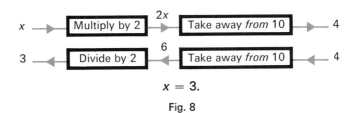

$$x = 3.$$

Fig. 8

Copy and complete Figure 9 for

$$4 - 3x = {}^-2.$$

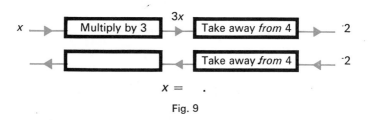

$$x = \quad .$$

Fig. 9

Dces your answer fit the equation?

Exercise D

Solve the following equations by using flow diagrams.

1 $8 - 2x = 2.$	2 $12 - 3x = 6.$
3 $14 - 4x = 4.$	4 $20 - 2x = {}^-2.$
5 $10 - 3x = 16.$	6 ${}^-6 - 2x = {}^-12.$
7 $5 - 3x = {}^-4.$	8 ${}^-8 - 4x = 10.$
9 $8 = 14 - 3x.$	10 $6 = 4 - 5x.$

1.6 All kinds of equations

The next exercise has examples of all the types of equations you have met so far. Solve them by drawing flow diagrams. (In Questions 1 and 2, be especially careful not to muddle $2x - 3 = 6$ with $3 - 2x = 6$.)

Exercise E (*Miscellaneous*)

1   $2x - 3 = 5.$ 2 $3 - 2x = 6.$

3   $2x + 5 = 11.$ 4 $2(x - 3) = 7.$

5   $15 - 2x = {}^-8.$ 6 $30 - 2x = 4.$

7   $2x - 5 = 11.$ 8 $5 - \dfrac{x}{2} = 11.$

9   $6 - x = 2.$ 10 $\frac{1}{2}(x + 5) = 11.$

11   $4 - 3x = {}^-6.$ 12 ${}^-4 - 3x = {}^-6.$

13   $4x - 3 = {}^-8.$ 14 ${}^-4x - 3 = {}^-8.$

15   $24 - 3x = 0.$ 16 $12 - 6x = {}^-2.$

17   ${}^-8 - 2x = 4.$ 18 ${}^-2x - 8 = 4.$

19   ${}^-3x + 6 = {}^-2.$ 20 ${}^-6 - 3x = {}^-2.$

2. METHOD B: INVERSE ELEMENTS

First, work through Exercise F which gives some more practice with negative numbers.

Exercise F

1   $5 + {}^-5.$ 2 $5 - 5.$ 3 $4 + {}^-6.$

4   ${}^-3 + {}^-5.$ 5 ${}^-3 + 6.$ 6 $8 + {}^-2.$

7   $3 \times \frac{1}{3}.$ 8 ${}^-\frac{1}{5} \times {}^-5.$ 9 $4 \times {}^-\frac{1}{2}.$

10   ${}^-5 \times {}^-2.$ 11 ${}^-\frac{1}{2} \times {}^-6.$ 12 ${}^-8 \times 3.$

Had you remembered that $5 - 5$ and $5 + {}^-5$ have the same result?

In the rest of this chapter you will find it easier to write expressions like $5-5$ as $5+{}^-5$.

For example, if you have the equation

$$x-5 = 6,$$

first write it as $\qquad x+{}^-5 = 6.$

If you have $\qquad 6-x = 4,$

write it as $\qquad 6+{}^-x = 4.$

2.1 Inverse elements under addition

When you are dealing with addition, 0 is called the *identity element*, because if 0 is added to any number, the number remains unchanged.

For example, $\qquad 8+0 = 8,$

$$6+0 = 6, \text{ etc.}$$

What number when added to 4 gives the *identity element?*

$^-4$ is called the *inverse element* for 4 under addition because

$$4+{}^-4 = 0.$$

What are the inverse elements under addition for

(*a*) 6; $\qquad\qquad$ (*b*) $^-7$; $\qquad\qquad$ (*c*) 10?

2.2 Solving simple equations

We can use the idea of inverse elements in solving equations. The flow diagrams in Figure 10 show how to use this idea to solve

$$x+3 = 5.$$

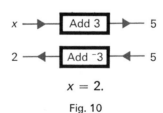

$$x = 2.$$

Fig. 10

In reversing the first flow diagram, we add $^-3$ because $^-3$ is the inverse element under addition for 3.

By Method A, the second flow diagram for this equation would have been:

$$2 \longleftarrow \boxed{\text{Take away 3}} \longleftarrow 5$$

'Add ⁻3' and 'take away 3' have the same effect, of course, so the two methods give the same answer.

If you have to solve $\qquad x - 6 = 4,$

first write it as $\qquad x + {}^-6 = 4.$

The flow diagrams are shown in Figure 11 :

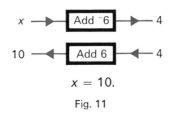

$$x \longrightarrow \boxed{\text{Add } ^-6} \longrightarrow 4$$

$$10 \longleftarrow \boxed{\text{Add } 6} \longleftarrow 4$$

$$x = 10.$$

Fig. 11

(Note that 6 is the inverse element for ⁻6 under addition.)

Draw your own flow diagrams for

$$x - 5 = {}^-3,$$

but first write it as $\qquad x + {}^-5 = {}^-3.$

Check that your answer fits the equation.

Exercise G

Solve the following equations, using the method of inverse elements. Even if you can spot the answers, draw the flow diagrams each time, so that you get used to the new ideas.

1 $x + 3 = 6.$

2 $x + 2 = {}^-3.$

3 $x + {}^-2 = 4.$

4 $x + {}^-3 = {}^-4.$

5 $x - 4 = 5.$

6 $x - 3 = {}^-7.$

7 $x - 7 = {}^-2.$

8 $x + 5 = {}^-8.$

111

2.3 Inverse elements under multiplication

In multiplying, the identity element is 1, because

$$6 \times 1 = 6,$$

$$8 \times 1 = 8, \text{ etc.}$$

$\frac{1}{4}$ is the inverse element for 4 under multiplication because $\frac{1}{4} \times 4 = 1.$

What are the inverse elements under multiplication for:

(a) 3;   (b) $\frac{1}{2}$;   (c) 6?

2.4 Equations such as 2x+3=7

We shall start by solving an easier example:

$$2x = 7.$$

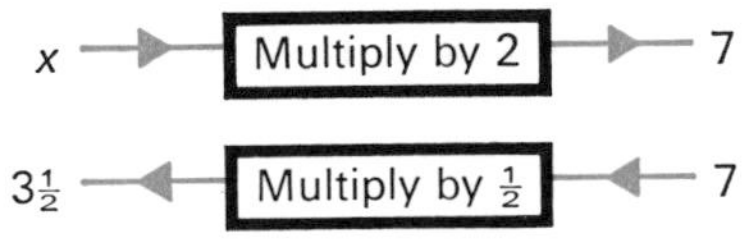

$$x \longrightarrow \boxed{\text{Multiply by 2}} \longrightarrow 7$$

$$3\tfrac{1}{2} \longleftarrow \boxed{\text{Multiply by } \tfrac{1}{2}} \longleftarrow 7$$

$$x = 3\tfrac{1}{2}.$$

Fig. 12

Copy and complete Figure 13 for

$$\tfrac{1}{2}x = {}^{-}3.$$

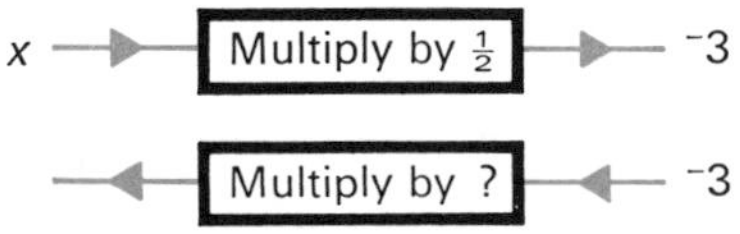

$$x \longrightarrow \boxed{\text{Multiply by } \tfrac{1}{2}} \longrightarrow {}^{-}3$$

$$\longleftarrow \boxed{\text{Multiply by ?}} \longleftarrow {}^{-}3$$

$$x = \quad .$$

Fig. 13

Check that your answer fits the equation.

Figure 14 now shows how to solve

$$2x+3 = 7.$$

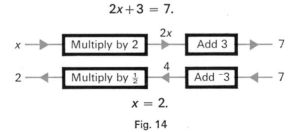

$$x = 2.$$

Fig. 14

Copy and complete Figure 15 to solve

$$3(x-2) = 9,$$

but first write it as $3(x+{}^-2) = 9.$

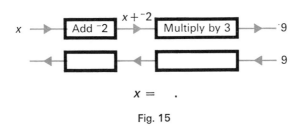

$$x = \quad .$$

Fig. 15

Check that your answer fits the equation.

Exercise H

Solve the following equations, using the method of inverse elements.

1   $2x+3 = 6.$
2   $2(x-1) = 8.$

3   $3x-5 = 7.$
4   $4(x+2) = 14.$

5   $3(2x-1) = {}^-9.$
6   $2(3x+4) = 10.$

7   $\frac{1}{2}x-2 = 5.$
8   $\frac{1}{3}(x+2) = 4.$

9   $3(\frac{1}{4}x-2) = 9.$
10   $\frac{1}{2}(2x+1) = 5.$

2.5   Equations with ´−2x´, ´−3x´, etc.

In this section you will need to work out the inverse elements under multiplication for negative numbers.

Since $-\frac{1}{2} \times {}^-2 = 1$, $-\frac{1}{2}$ is the inverse element for $^-2$ under multiplication.

What are the inverse elements under multiplication for:

(a) $^-4$;
(b) $-\frac{1}{3}$;
(c) $^-1$?

113

We can now solve equations like $10 - 2x = 4$ by using inverse elements:

We first write $10 - 2x = 4$

as $10 + {}^-2x = 4$

or ${}^-2x + 10 = 4.$

We then use flow diagrams:

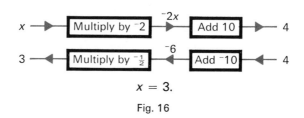

$$x = 3.$$

Fig. 16

Figure 17 shows the flow diagrams for

$$^-5 - 4x = 3,$$

which we write as $^-5 + {}^-4x = 3$

or $^-4x + {}^-5 = 3.$

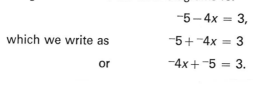

$$x = {}^-2.$$

Fig. 17

Copy and complete Figure 18 to solve

$$4 - 3x = {}^-2$$

$$4 + {}^-3x = {}^-2$$

$${}^-3x + 4 = {}^-2.$$

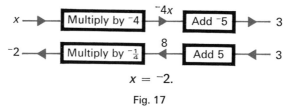

$$x = \quad .$$

Fig. 18

Does your answer fit the equation?

Exercise I

Solve the following equations, using the method of inverse elements.

1   $8 - 2x = 2.$

2   $12 - 3x = 6.$

3   $14 - 4x = 4.$

4   $20 - 2x = {}^-2.$

5   $10 - 3x = 16.$

6   ${}^-6 - 2x = {}^-12.$

7   $5 - 3x = {}^-4.$

8   ${}^-8 - 4x = 10.$

9   $4 - \frac{1}{2}x = 2.$

10   ${}^-6 - \frac{1}{4}x = {}^-2.$

2.6   Equations with ' $-x$ '

We shall now see how to solve equations such as

$$6 - x = 2$$

or $\qquad\qquad 6 + {}^-x = 2.$

Since ${}^-x$ means the same as ${}^-1x$, we can write $6 + {}^-x = 2$ as

$$6 + {}^-1x = 2$$

or $\qquad\qquad {}^-1x + 6 = 2.$

The flow diagrams for solving ${}^-1x + 6 = 2$ are as follows :

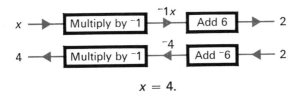

$$x = 4.$$

Fig. 19

Did you remember that the inverse element for ${}^-1$ under multiplication is ${}^-1$?

Now copy and complete Figure 20 to solve

$$^-2 - x = 4$$
$$^-2 + {^-1}x = 4$$
$$^-1x + {^-2} = 4.$$

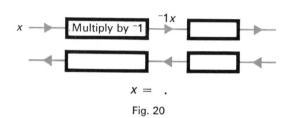

$$x = \quad .$$

Fig. 20

Check that your answer fits the equation.

Exercise J

Solve the following equations by using this method. Show the working and draw a flow diagram each time.

1 $7 - x = 2.$ 2 $4 - x = {^-3}.$

3 $3 - x = 5.$ 4 $2 - x = {^-4}.$

5 $13 - x = {^-2}.$ 6 $^-2 - x = 4.$

7 $^-3 - x = 2.$ 8 $^-4 - x = {^-3}.$

9 $4 = 6 - x.$ 10 $5 = 3 - x.$

Solve the equations in Exercise K by using the method of inverse elements. Remember that for equations such as $6 - x = 2$ or $3 - 2x = 6$ you must re-arrange the equation before you draw the flow diagrams.

Exercise K (*Miscellaneous*)

1 $2x - 3 = 6.$ 2 $3 - 2x = 6.$

3 $2x + 5 = 11.$ 4 $2(x - 3) = 7.$

5 $12 - 5x = {^-8}.$ 6 $30 - \frac{1}{2}x = 24.$

7 $6 - x = 2.$ 8 $5 + 2x = 11.$

9 $\frac{1}{2}x + 5 = 11.$ 10 $\frac{1}{2}(x + 5) = 11.$

11 $4 - 3x = {}^-6.$ 12 ${}^-4 - 3x = {}^-6.$

13 $4x - 3 = {}^-8.$ 14 ${}^-4x - 3 = {}^-8.$

15 $24 - 3x = 0.$ 16 $12 - 6x = {}^-2.$

17 ${}^-8 - 2x = 4.$ 18 ${}^-2x - 8 = 4.$

19 ${}^-3x + 6 = {}^-2.$ 20 ${}^-6 - 3x = {}^-2.$

10. Matrices at work: transformations

(a) The vertices of the triangle in Figure 1 are A (1, 3), B (1, 1) and C (2, 1).

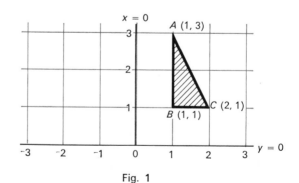

Fig. 1

The journey from the origin to A can be written as the 2 by 1 matrix $\begin{pmatrix} 1 \\ 3 \end{pmatrix}$ (see Figure 2).

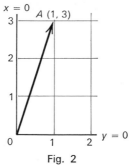

Fig. 2

The journeys from the origin to B and from the origin to C are shown in Figures 3 and 4. Write each of these journeys as 2 by 1 matrices.

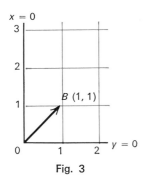

Fig. 3

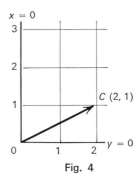

Fig. 4

We shall now try to find out what happens to these journeys when we multiply them by another matrix on the left, for example, the matrix

$$\mathbf{M} = \begin{pmatrix} -1 & 0 \\ 0 & 1 \end{pmatrix}.$$

Copy and complete each of these multiplications:

$$\overset{A}{\begin{pmatrix} -1 & 0 \\ 0 & 1 \end{pmatrix}} \overset{}{\begin{pmatrix} 1 \\ 3 \end{pmatrix}} = \overset{A'}{\begin{pmatrix} -1 \\ \ \end{pmatrix}};$$

$$\begin{pmatrix} -1 & 0 \\ 0 & 1 \end{pmatrix} \overset{B}{\begin{pmatrix} 1 \\ 1 \end{pmatrix}} = \overset{B'}{\begin{pmatrix} -1 \\ \ \end{pmatrix}};$$

$$\begin{pmatrix} -1 & 0 \\ 0 & 1 \end{pmatrix} \overset{C}{\begin{pmatrix} 2 \\ 1 \end{pmatrix}} = \overset{C'}{\begin{pmatrix} \ \\ \ \end{pmatrix}}.$$

The matrix **M** changes or transforms the journeys

$$\begin{pmatrix}1\\3\end{pmatrix}, \quad \begin{pmatrix}1\\1\end{pmatrix} \quad \text{and} \quad \begin{pmatrix}2\\1\end{pmatrix}$$

into the journeys

$$\begin{pmatrix}-1\\3\end{pmatrix}, \quad \begin{pmatrix}-1\\1\end{pmatrix} \quad \text{and} \quad \begin{pmatrix}-2\\1\end{pmatrix}.$$

We therefore have:

Original point	Journey	Transformed journey	Transformed point
A (1, 3)	$\begin{pmatrix}1\\3\end{pmatrix}$	$\begin{pmatrix}-1\\3\end{pmatrix}$	A' ($^-$1, 3)
B (1, 1)	$\begin{pmatrix}1\\1\end{pmatrix}$	$\begin{pmatrix}-1\\1\end{pmatrix}$	B' ($^-$1, 1)
C (2, 1)	$\begin{pmatrix}2\\1\end{pmatrix}$	$\begin{pmatrix}-2\\1\end{pmatrix}$	C' ($^-$2, 1)

Copy Figure 1 and draw the transformed triangle $A'B'C'$. What is the effect of multiplying the journeys to A, B and C by the matrix **M** on the left? What transformation does **M** represent?

Instead of writing each journey separately, we can show all three journeys in a single matrix:

$$\begin{matrix} A & B & C \\ \begin{pmatrix}1 & 1 & 2\\3 & 1 & 1\end{pmatrix} \end{matrix}.$$

We can then multiply this single matrix by

$$\mathbf{M} = \begin{pmatrix}-1 & 0\\0 & 1\end{pmatrix}$$

on the left. Copy and complete this multiplication:

$$\begin{pmatrix}-1 & 0\\0 & 1\end{pmatrix} \begin{matrix} A & B & C \\ \begin{pmatrix}1 & 1 & 2\\3 & 1 & 1\end{pmatrix} \end{matrix} = \begin{matrix} A' & B' & C' \\ \begin{pmatrix}-1 & -1 & \\3 & & \end{pmatrix} \end{matrix}.$$

As before, we see that **M** transforms the journeys

$$\begin{pmatrix}1\\3\end{pmatrix}, \quad \begin{pmatrix}1\\1\end{pmatrix} \quad \text{and} \quad \begin{pmatrix}2\\1\end{pmatrix}$$

into the journeys

$$\begin{pmatrix}-1\\3\end{pmatrix}, \quad \begin{pmatrix}-1\\1\end{pmatrix} \quad \text{and} \quad \begin{pmatrix}-2\\1\end{pmatrix}.$$

(b) Draw axes on squared paper. Draw a triangle of your own (choose whole number coordinates for the vertices) and call it *PQR*.

Write down the 2 by 1 matrices which describe the journeys from the origin to *P*, *Q* and *R*. Now write these journeys as a single matrix and multiply this matrix by

$$\mathbf{M} = \begin{pmatrix} -1 & 0 \\ 0 & 1 \end{pmatrix}$$

on the left.

Let *P'*, *Q'*, *R'* be the images of *P*, *Q*, *R*. Draw triangle *P'Q'R'*.

Describe the transformation which maps triangle *PQR* onto triangle *P'Q'R'*. We say that the matrix **M** represents this transformation.

(c) Multiply **M** by itself, that is, find $\mathbf{M}^2$. What is the effect of multiplying the journeys to *P*, *Q* and *R* by the matrix $\mathbf{M}^2$ on the left?

What two transformations does $\mathbf{M}^2$ represent?

What single transformation does $\mathbf{M}^2$ represent?

Exercise A

1 The matrix

$$\mathbf{J} = \begin{matrix} O & L & M & N \\ \begin{pmatrix} 0 & 2 & 3 & 3 \\ 0 & 1 & 1 & 0 \end{pmatrix} \end{matrix}$$

shows the journeys from the origin to the vertices of the quadrilateral *OLMN* in Figure 5.

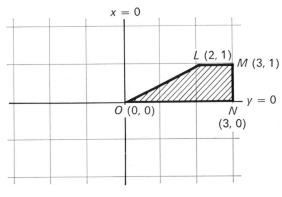

Fig. 5

(a) Multiply **J** by the matrix $\begin{pmatrix} -1 & 0 \\ 0 & -1 \end{pmatrix}$ on the left.

(*b*) On a diagram show the quadrilateral *OLMN* and its image after the transformation represented by

$$\begin{pmatrix} -1 & 0 \\ 0 & -1 \end{pmatrix}.$$

(*c*) Describe the transformation which $\begin{pmatrix} -1 & 0 \\ 0 & -1 \end{pmatrix}$ represents.

Repeat Question 1 replacing the matrix $\begin{pmatrix} -1 & 0 \\ 0 & -1 \end{pmatrix}$ by each of the following six matrices:

2 $\begin{pmatrix} 0 & -1 \\ 1 & 0 \end{pmatrix}.$ 3 $\begin{pmatrix} 1 & 0 \\ 0 & -1 \end{pmatrix}.$ 4 $\begin{pmatrix} 0 & -1 \\ -1 & 0 \end{pmatrix}.$

5 $\begin{pmatrix} 1 & 0 \\ 0 & 1 \end{pmatrix}.$ 6 $\begin{pmatrix} 2 & 0 \\ 0 & 2 \end{pmatrix}.$ 7 $\begin{pmatrix} -3 & 0 \\ 0 & -3 \end{pmatrix}.$

8 (*a*) Look at Figure 6. Write down a 2 by 4 matrix to show the journeys from the origin to *E, F, G* and *H*. Call it **K**.

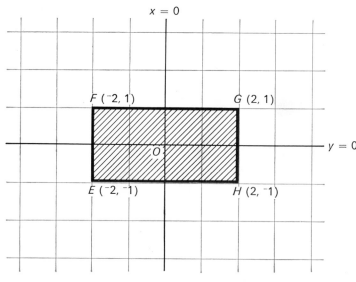

Fig. 6

(*b*) Multiply **K** by the matrix $\begin{pmatrix} 2 & 0 \\ 0 & 1 \end{pmatrix}$ on the left.

(*c*) On a diagram, show the rectangle *EFGH* and its image after the transformation represented by

$$\begin{pmatrix} 2 & 0 \\ 0 & 1 \end{pmatrix}.$$

(*d*) Try to describe the transformation which

$$\begin{pmatrix} 2 & 0 \\ 0 & 1 \end{pmatrix}$$

represents. If you have any difficulty, find the effect of this matrix on some other shapes. (You are advised to choose whole number coordinates for the vertices.)

9 Repeat Question 8 replacing the matrix

$$\begin{pmatrix} 2 & 0 \\ 0 & 1 \end{pmatrix} \text{ by the matrix } \begin{pmatrix} 1 & 0 \\ 0 & 3 \end{pmatrix}.$$

10 Repeat Question 8 replacing the matrix

$$\begin{pmatrix} 2 & 0 \\ 0 & 1 \end{pmatrix} \text{ by the matrix } \begin{pmatrix} 2 & 0 \\ 0 & 3 \end{pmatrix}.$$

11 If $A = \begin{pmatrix} 0 & 1 \\ -1 & 0 \end{pmatrix}$, work out A^2, A^3 and A^4.

Describe the transformations represented by A, A^2, A^3 and A^4 by drawing a shape of your own and finding what effect each of these matrices has on it. Try to explain your results.

What would A^5 represent? What would A^{16} represent?

12 If
$$B = \begin{pmatrix} 0 & 1 \\ 1 & 0 \end{pmatrix},$$

describe the transformations represented by B, B^2, B^3 and B^4. Try to explain your results.

What would B^6 represent? What would B^{19} represent?

13 Draw a triangle *ABC* on squared paper. Write down a 2 by 3 matrix to show the journeys from the origin to *A*, *B*, and *C*.

Multiply this matrix by $\begin{pmatrix} 0 & 1 \\ -1 & 0 \end{pmatrix}$ on the left.

Now multiply the result by $\begin{pmatrix} 0 & -1 \\ 1 & 0 \end{pmatrix}$ on the left.

What has happened to your triangle? Find a single matrix which represents this transformation.

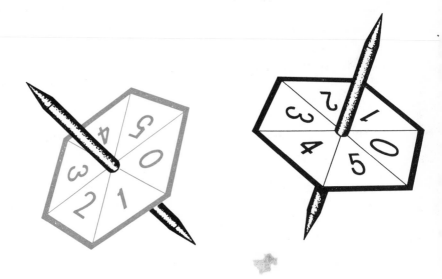

11. Problems and their solution sets

1. SOLUTION SETS

The drawing at the head of the chapter shows two hexagonal spinners, one red and one black, numbered from 0 to 5. Suppose we spin both spinners together. We can show all the possible outcomes on a graph (see Figure 1).

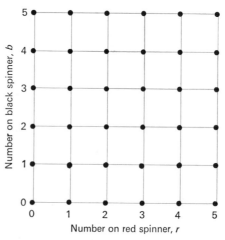

Fig. 1

(*a*) The ordered pair (1, 3) means a '1' on the red spinner and a '3' on the black spinner. What does (3, 1) mean?

(*b*) The ordered pair (1, 3) gives a total score of 4. What possible scores can we get when we spin both spinners? List these scores.

(*c*) In how many ways could we score a total of 4? On a copy of Figure 1, put a small circle round each point which represents a score of 4. What do you notice?

On another copy of Figure 1, put a small circle round each point which represents a score of 7. Do these points lie on a straight line?

(*d*) Alan is playing a game. It is his turn and he needs 7 or more to win. The set of all possible outcomes which would give Alan a score of at least 7 is called his *solution set*.

Write down the ordered pairs which belong to Alan's solution set. On a copy of Figure 1, put a small circle round each point which represents a member of this set. How many members has it?

(*e*) We can let r stand for the number on the red spinner and b stand for the number on the black spinner. What does $r+b$ stand for?

Figure 2 shows Alan's solution set. This is the set of points such that $r+b$ is more than or equal to 7 or, more briefly, the points for which

$$r+b \geqslant 7.$$

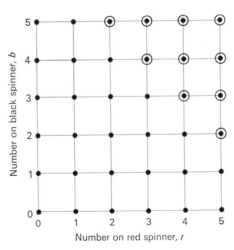

Fig. 2. $r+b \geqslant 7$.

If we wish to score exactly 7, then our solution set is the set of points for which $$r+b = 7.$$

What is our solution set if we wish to score 7 or less?

(*f*) What is our solution set if we wish to score:
   (i)   exactly 4;
   (ii) at least 4;
   (iii) 4 or less?

(*g*) On a copy of Figure 1, put a small circle round each member of the set of points for which
$$6 \leqslant r+b \leqslant 8.$$

Describe this set in words.

(*h*) Figure 3 shows the set of points for which

$$r = b+2.$$

List the ordered pairs which belong to this set. Describe the set in words.

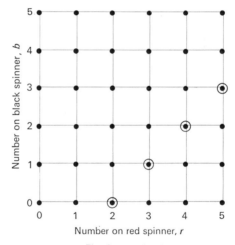

Fig. 3. $r = b+2.$

What is the solution set if we want the number on the red spinner to be *at least* two more than the number on the black spinner?
Draw a graph of this set. How many members has it?

Exercise A

Answer each part of Questions 1, 2 and 3 on a separate copy of Figure 1.

1 (*a*) Draw a graph of the set of points for which $r+b = 6$, that is, show the set of ways in which a total of 6 can be scored.

(*b*) Draw a graph of the set of points for which $r+b \leqslant 6$. Describe the set in words.

(*c*) Draw a graph of the set of points for which $r+b \geqslant 3$. Describe the set in words.

(*d*) Draw a graph of the set of points for which $3 \leqslant r+b \leqslant 6$. Describe the set in words.

2 (*a*) Brenda wishes to score a total of 5 or less. Draw her solution set. Label your graph $r+b \leqslant 5$.

(*b*) Charles wishes to score a total of 8 or more. Draw his solution set. Label your graph.

(*c*) Diana wishes to score at least 2 but not more than 7. Draw her solution set. Label your graph.

3 Draw a graph of each of the following sets. Then describe each set in words.

(*a*) The set of points for which $r = b+1$.
(*b*) The set of points for which $r = b$.
(*c*) The set of points for which $r \leqslant b$.
(*d*) The set of points for which $r \geqslant b+4$.
(*e*) The set of points for which $r = b-2$.

4 In a dancing class there are 10 men and 10 women but they do not always all attend. If more men go than women, some men will be without a partner. If there are more women than men, some women will be without a partner. For example, if 8 women and 6 men attend, 2 women will be without a partner.

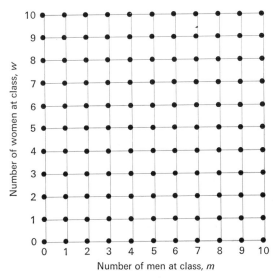

Fig. 4

(*a*) On a copy of Figure 4, put a small circle round each point which represents a way of having 2 women without a partner.

Let *m* stand for the number of men at the class and *w* for the number of women at the class. Label your graph.

(*b*) On another copy of Figure 4, put a small circle round those points which represent ways of having at least 3 men without a partner. Label your graph.

(*c*) Draw a graph of the set of points for which $m \geqslant w$. Describe this set in words.

(*d*) One day at the class, no-one is without a partner. In how many ways can this happen? Draw a graph to show these ways. Label your graph.

5   A box contains 7 red beads and 4 blue ones. If a red bead is taken from the box, 1 point is scored. If a blue one is taken, 2 points are scored. A turn consists of taking some beads from the box.

(*a*) If 2 red beads and 3 blue beads are taken, how many points are scored?

(*b*) If 3 red beads and 2 blue beads are taken, how many points are scored?

(*c*) Let *r* stand for the number of red beads taken and *b* stand for the number of blue beads taken. 1 point is scored for each red bead, so *r* points are scored for the *r* red beads. 2 points are scored for each blue bead, so 2*b* points are scored for the *b* blue beads. How many points are scored altogether?

(*d*) On a copy of Figure 5, draw a graph of the points for which $r + 2b = 7$, that is, show the ways of scoring exactly 7 points. What do you notice?

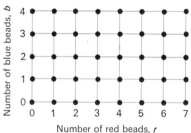

Fig. 5

(*e*) Draw a graph to show the ways in which 4 points can be scored. Label your graph.

(*f*) Draw a graph to show the ways of scoring at least 9. Label your graph.

(*g*) Draw a graph of the set of points for which $r + 2b \leqslant 2$. Describe this set in words.

2. GRAPHING RELATIONS

Figure 1 shows the 36 points which represent the possible outcomes when we spin the red and black spinners together.

(*a*) On a copy of Figure 1, put a small circle round each point which represents a score of 7. How should you label your graph?

Your points should lie on a straight line. On another copy of Figure 1, draw this line. Put a small circle round those points which lie on or above the line. Compare your graph with that in Figure 2. How should you label your graph?

Draw your line on another copy of Figure 1. This time put a small circle round each point which lies on or below the line. Try to label your graph.

(*b*) Check that the straight line in Figure 6 is drawn through the points which represent a score of 4, that is, the points which fit the relation $r + b = 4$.

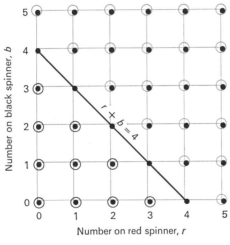

Fig. 6

The points below the line are marked with a black circle. Find the value of $r + b$ at each of these points and check that they fit the relation $r + b < 4$.

The points above the line are marked with a red circle. Find the value of $r + b$ at each of these points and check that they fit the relation $r + b > 4$.

The method of graphing solution sets which we used in Section 1 can be rather tedious. We can use the idea that points on one side of the line $r + b = 4$ fit the relation $r + b < 4$ and that points on the other side fit the relation $r + b > 4$ to draw them more quickly.

(*c*) Suppose we want the number on the red spinner to be less than the number on the black spinner. We want the set of points which fit the relation *r* < *b*.

On a copy of Figure 1, draw a straight line through the points which fit the relation *r* = *b*.

Choose a point in the region above the line, for example the point (2, 5). Does it fit the relation *r* > *b* or *r* < *b*?

Now choose a point in the region below the line. Does it fit the relation *r* > *b* or *r* < *b*?

Shade out the region which you do *not* want and put a small circle round each point in the region which you do want. Label your graph *r* < *b*.

The points on the line *r* = *b* do not belong to the solution set. Why not?

Compare your graph with that in Figure 7.

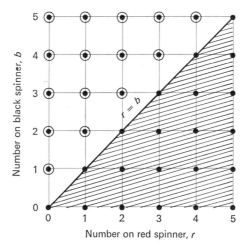

Fig. 7. *r* < *b*.

(*d*) Now suppose we want the number on the red spinner to be less than or equal to the number on the black spinner. We now need the set of points which fit the relation *r* ⩽ *b*. Draw a graph of the solution set.

Do the points on the line *r* = *b* belong to the solution set?

(*e*) Suppose we want the number on the red spinner to be *at least* two more than the number on the black spinner. We need the set of points which fit the relation *r* ⩾ *b*+2.

The set of points for which *r* = *b*+2 is shown in Figure 3. Do these points belong to the solution set?

Copy Figure 3 and draw a straight line through these points. Label the line $r = b + 2$.

Choose a point in the region above the line, for example, the point (1, 4). Find the values of r and $b + 2$ at this point. Does it fit the relation $r > b + 2$ or $r < b + 2$?

Now choose a point in the region below the line. Find the values of r and $b + 2$ at this point. Does it fit the relation $r > b + 2$ or $r < b + 2$?

Shade out the region which you do *not* want and put a small circle round each point in the region which you do want. Label your graph $r \geqslant b + 2$.

Compare your graph with the one you drew for Section 1 part (*h*).

(*f*) Draw a graph to show the relation $r < b + 2$.

(*g*) If you were unable to label any of the graphs which you drew in part (*a*), go back and label them now.

Exercise B

Use the method of Section 2 to answer the questions in this exercise.

1 On separate copies of Figure 1, draw graphs to show each of the following relations.

    (*a*) $r + b > 5$;   (*b*) $r + b < 5$;

    (*c*) $r + b \geqslant 5$;   (*d*) $r + b \leqslant 5$.

2 On separate copies of Figure 1, draw graphs to show each of the following relations.

    (*a*) $r > b + 1$;   (*b*) $r \leqslant b + 3$;   (*c*) $r > b - 2$.

3 In a dancing class there are 10 men and 10 women but they do not always all attend. m stands for the number of men at the class and w for the number of women at the class.

    Draw a graph of the set of points which fit each of the following relations. Draw each graph on a separate copy of Figure 4 and then describe the set in words.

    (*a*) $m + w \geqslant 7$;   (*b*) $m \geqslant 8$;

    (*c*) $w < 3$;   (*d*) $m < 5$;

    (*e*) $m \geqslant w$;   (*f*) $m \geqslant w + 2$.

4 At another dancing class there are 8 men and 8 women but again the
do not always all attend. *m* stands for the number of men at the clas
and *w* for the number of women at the class.

Draw a graph of the set of points which fit each of the followin
relations. Then try to describe the set in words.

(a) $m \geqslant 2w$;   (b) $3m \leqslant w$.

5 A box contains 7 red beads and 4 blue ones. If a red bead is taken fror
the box, 1 point is scored. If a blue one is taken, 2 points are scorec
A turn consists of taking some beads from the box.

(a) If *r* is the number of red beads taken and *b* is the number of blu
beads taken, explain why $r + 2b$ gives the total score. If you hav
difficulty, look at Exercise A, Question 5.

(b) List the ways in which a total of 6 can be scored. Use these t
help you to draw the line $r + 2b = 6$ on a copy of Figure 5.

(c) Draw a graph of the set of points which fit the relation $r + 2b \geqslant 6$
Describe this set in words.

(d) Draw a graph to show the set of ways of scoring at least 9. Labe
your graph.

3. SOLVING PROBLEMS

A ferry transports cars and buses. The ferry has 12 car-spaces and a bu
takes up the space of 3 cars. How many cars and buses can the ferry tak
on one crossing?

There are, of course, many different answers to this problem. Fc
example, the ferry could take 6 cars and 2 buses or it could take 1 ca
and 1 bus and have 8 empty spaces. What is the largest number of car
the ferry could take? What is the largest number of buses?

Let *c* stand for the number of cars taken on the crossing and *b* for th
number of buses.

Each car occupies 1 space, so *c* cars need *c* spaces. Each bus occupie
3 spaces, so *b* buses need $3b$ spaces. Explain why $c + 3b$ gives the tota
number of *occupied* car-spaces.

The ferry has only 12 spaces, so we need the set of points in Figure 8 for which $c + 3b \leqslant 12$.

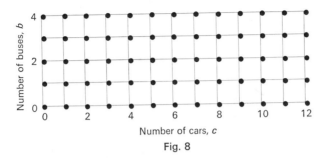

Fig. 8

By now you will probably have realized that the points which fit the relation $c + 3b = 12$ lie on a straight line. Therefore we need find only two points which fit this relation, but it is sensible to find a third as a check.

We already know three ways of occupying all 12 car-spaces:

> 0 cars and 4 buses,
> 6 cars and 2 buses,
> 12 cars and 0 buses.

So the points (0, 4), (6, 2) and (12, 0) fit the relation $c + 3b = 12$.

Mark these points on a copy of Figure 8 and draw a straight line through them. Label the line $c + 3b = 12$.

Choose a point above the line and find the value of $c + 3b$ at this point. Does it fit the relation $c + 3b > 12$ or $c + 3b < 12$?

Now choose a point below the line and find the value of $c + 3b$ at this point. Does it fit the relation $c + 3b > 12$ or $c + 3b < 12$? Shade out the region which you do *not* want and put a small circle round each point in the region you do want. Do the points on the line belong to the solution set? If so, put a circle round these points also. Label your graph $c + 3b \leqslant 12$. How many members does the solution set have?

Compare your graph with that in Figure 9.

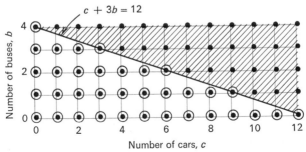

Fig. 9. $c + 3b \leqslant 12$.

Exercise C

1   John has 18p. He goes to a baker's shop which sells only doughnuts
and buns. Buns cost 1p each and doughnuts cost 3p each.

(*a*) What is the largest number of buns which John can buy? What
is the largest number of doughnuts?

(*b*) If John buys 2 buns and 4 doughnuts, how much does he spend?

(*c*) Suppose John buys *b* buns and *d* doughnuts. *b* buns cost *b* pence
and *d* doughnuts cost 3*d* pence, so John spends *b*+3*d* pence
altogether. Explain why $b+3d \leqslant 18$.

(*d*) Write down three ways in which John could spend *all* his money
and show these ways by marking 3 points on a copy of Figure 10.
These points should lie on a straight line. Draw this line and label it
$b+3d = 18$.

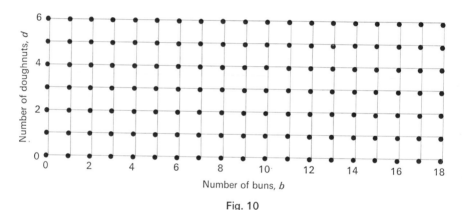

Fig. 10

(*e*) By shading out the unwanted region, draw a graph of John's
solution set. Label it $b+3d \leqslant 18$.

(*f*) In how many different ways could John
   (i) spend all his money;
   (ii) not spend all his money?

2   Fred goes to a fair with 24p in his pocket. He is interested only in the
coconut shy which costs 3p a turn and the rifle range which costs 4p
a turn.

(*a*) What is the largest number of turns which Fred could have at
(i) the coconut shy; (ii) the rifle range?

(*b*) If Fred has 2 turns at the coconut shy and 3 turns at the rifle range,
how much money does he spend?

(*c*) *c* turns at the coconut shy cost 3*c* pence and *r* turns at the rifle range cost 4*r* pence. If Fred has *c* turns at the coconut shy and *r* turns at the rifle range, he will spend $3c + 4r$ pence altogether. Explain why $3c + 4r \leqslant 24$.

(*d*) Write down three ways in which Fred could spend *all* his money. Show these ways by marking 3 points on a copy of Figure 11. Draw a straight line through these points and label it $3c + 4r = 24$.

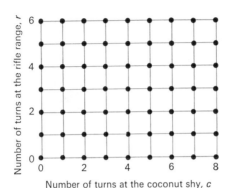

Fig. 11

(*e*) By shading out the unwanted region, draw a graph of Fred's solution set. Label your graph.

(*f*) In how many different ways could Fred spend all his money?

3 Jane goes to a fair with 60p in her pocket. She has *d* rides on the dodgems and *r* rides on the rockets. Dodgems cost 5p a ride and rockets cost 6p a ride.

(*a*) *d* rides on the dodgems cost 5*d* pence and *r* rides on the rockets cost 6*r* pence, so Jane spends $5d + 6r$ pence. Explain why $5d + 6r \leqslant 60$.

(*b*) Find three ways in which Jane could spend all her money and use these to draw the line $5d + 6r = 60$.

(*c*) Draw a graph of Jane's solution set. Label your graph.

(*d*) In how many different ways could Jane spend some or all of her money?

12. Computers and programming

In the last twenty years, machines have been developed which can perform complicated calculations very quickly. These machines are called *computers*.

How long would it take you to do the following problems?

(*a*) Find the square root of 2, to 4 decimal places.

(*b*) Work out $\dfrac{37 \cdot 2 \times 0 \cdot 817}{568}$.

(*c*) Find the mean age of your class.

A computer could solve these problems in a fraction of a second. However, before it could begin, it would have to be told exactly what to do—computers are completely stupid, but they are very good at doing what they are told, and doing it quickly.

Try to find out as much as you can about computers. For example,

(*a*) what types of problems they can solve;

(*b*) how they work;

(*c*) what effect they could have on our lives in the future.

1. SIMON, THE HUMAN COMPUTER

In order to explain how a computer works we are going to describe an imaginary computer. Most computers have names; ours is called SIMON. Although Simon is an imaginary computer, the only differences between Simon and a real computer are that Simon is very much simpler and slower and has people acting as its various parts.

To make Simon you will need:

> Three large boxes (shoe or chalk boxes).
> Eight small boxes (match-boxes).

Decide among yourselves who is to play the part of:

(*a*) the storekeeper;

(*b*) the calculator (sometimes called the arithmetic unit);

(*c*) the controller;

(*d*) the machine operator.

The first three people must arrange themselves as shown in Figure 1 with the controller seated at one desk, the store on his right and the arithmetic unit on his left. The machine operator sits out of the way and watches the others work.

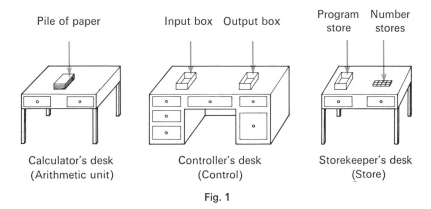

Calculator's desk   Controller's desk   Storekeeper's desk
(Arithmetic unit)   (Control)   (Store)

Fig. 1

The storekeeper labels the small boxes *A, B, C, D, E, F, G* and *H*. He will use these to store numbers in. He also needs one of the large boxes.

The calculator must have some paper to work on.

The controller takes the two remaining boxes and labels them *Input* and *Output*.

The computer is now waiting to be told what to do. The machine operator must write a set of instructions for the machine to carry out.

This set of instructions is called the *program*. It must be written in a language which the machine can understand. Simon's language is called *Simpol*.

Here is a program for Simon written in Simpol:

(1) Input to *A*.
(2) Input to *B*.
(3) Input to *C*.
(4) Input to *D*.
(5) Replace *E* by *A*+*B*.
(6) Replace *F* by *C*+*D*.
(7) Replace *G* by *E*+*F*.
(8) Replace *H* by *G*÷4.
(9) Output from *H*.

The machine operator copies this program onto a sheet of paper and puts it into the input box. The controller passes the program to the store-keeper who looks after it.

The operator must now decide what numbers he wants the program to work with. For our program we need four numbers; let us suppose that the operator chooses 2, 6, 7 and 33. He must then write each number on a separate piece of paper and place the four pieces of paper, in order, in the input box (with the first number on top of the pile).

The computer is now ready to go to work on the program.

The controller asks the storekeeper for the first instruction on the program and is told

(1) Input to *A*.

This tells the controller to pass the first number in the input box to the storekeeper who places it in the store labelled *A*.

The instructions numbered (2), (3) and (4) are carried out in a similar manner. The contents of the stores should now look like this:

A	B	C	D	E	F	G	H
2	6	7	33				

The controller now asks for the next instruction and is told

(5) Replace *E* by *A*+*B*.

The controller asks the storekeeper what numbers are held in stores *A* and *B*. He makes a copy of these numbers (2 and 6) and passes them to the calculator with the instruction that they are to be added together. The calculator writes the answer down and passes it back to the controller who gives it to the storekeeper telling him to store the answer in *E*.

The rest of the program is worked in a similar manner until we reach the last instruction:

(9) Output from *H*.

The controller asks for a copy of the number which the storekeeper has in store *H* and places this number in the output box where it is collected by the machine operator.

Run the same program again but use four different numbers.

What calculation does this particular program carry out?

2. REAL COMPUTERS

Simon, the human computer, is very slow, but he does work in the same way as a real computer.

A real computer consists of the same basic units:

Storage unit
Arithmetic unit
Control unit
Input unit
Output unit.

Like Simon, a real computer would also have two types of inputs: the numbers or *data* as they are called, and the program instructions. The numbers are punched, in binary, on tape or cards. The instructions are also put on tape or cards using a special binary code.

Figure 2 shows the connection between these units. Check that Simon works in the same way.

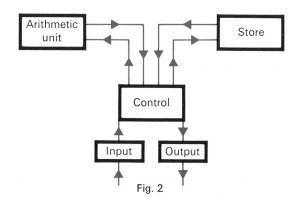

Fig. 2

Find out further details about each unit of a real computer.

3. CHECKING PROGRAMS

In order to check programs, each member of the class can act as a complete Simon instead of using a different person for each unit. All the working can be done in a table, as shown below, by putting the numbers in the appropriate columns as you work through the program.

Copy the table and use the program on p. 138 to complete it. The inputs have already been filled in and instructions (5) and (6) have been carried out. You should finish up with the answer 12 in column *H*.

A	B	C	D	E	F	G	H
2	6	7	33	8	40		

4. ALLOWABLE INSTRUCTIONS

(*a*) You should have found that the program you have been using calculated the mean of four numbers. You might have thought that it would be quicker to say to Simon

Replace *E* by $(A+B+C+D) \div 4$,

instead of using the four instructions numbered (5), (6), (7) and (8). But this is against the rules for Simon: he is only allowed to do one operation (such as addition or division) at a time.

How many instructions would be needed to work out

$$3 \times 4 \times 5 \times 6,$$

assuming that the numbers were already in Simon's stores?

(*b*) An instruction like:

Replace *E* by *A* + *B*

means that the numbers in stores *A* and *B* are added together and the result is put into store *E*. If there was already a number, 125 say, in store *E* then it would be removed automatically. Notice, however, that the numbers in stores *A* and *B* remain there. For example,

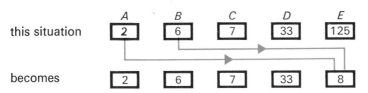

this situation

becomes

Draw similar diagrams, beginning in each case with the numbers 2, 6, 7, 33, 125, to show the results of the following instructions:

(1) Replace *E* by *B* × *C*.
(2) Replace *A* by *A* + *B*.
(3) Replace *B* by *B* ÷ *A*.
(4) Replace *D* by *D* − *C*.
(5) Replace *A* by *A* + *A*.

Exercise A

In this exercise remember not to write in your text book, but to make copies of all the tables.

1   Work through the following program with the numbers 2, 6, 7, 33. Like the program on p. 138, this one also works out the mean of four numbers. Has this program any advantages over the previous one?

	A	B	C	D
Input to *A*.	2			
Input to *B*.		6		
Input to *C*.			7	
Input to *D*.				33
Replace *A* by *A* + *B*.				
Replace *A* by *A* + *C*.				
Replace *A* by *A* + *D*.				
Replace *A* by *A* ÷ 4.				
Output from *A*.				

2   Follow through these programs:

(a)

A	B	C	D	E
5				
	3			
		4		

Input to *A*.
Input to *B*.
Input to *C*.
Replace *D* by *A − B*.
Replace *E* by *C × D*.
Output from *E*.

(b)

A	B	C	D	E	F	G
23						
	25					
		18				
			6			

Input to *A*.
Input to B.
Input to *C*.
Input to *D*.
Replace *E* by *A + B*.
Replace *F* by *C − D*.
Replace *G* by *E ÷ F*.
Output from *G*.

3   Write a program to find the mean of three numbers.
    Check it with the numbers 7, 9, 11.

4   Write a program to find the area of a triangle whose base is of length
    6 cm, and whose height is 8 cm.

5   Write a program to find the volume of a cuboid whose dimensions are
    7 cm, 9 cm and 12 cm.

6   (a) Work through this program:

A	B
2	

Input to *A*.
Replace *B* by *A × A*.
Replace *B* by *A × B*.
Replace *B* by *A × B*.
Output from *B*.

(*b*) Write a program which also computes 2^4 but uses fewer instructions.

(*c*) Write a program to compute 3^6.

7 The following program was intended to compute $4^2 + 5^2$, but there is a mistake in it. Correct it. What does this program actually compute?

A	B	C
4		
	5	

Input to *A*.
Input to *B*.
Replace *C* by $A + B$.
Replace *C* by $C \times C$.
Output from *C*.

8 A girl wishes to buy a bicycle. She buys it on H.P. paying a deposit of £5 and then £0·70 per week for 52 weeks. If she had bought it straight off it would have cost £35.

Write a program which will compute how much extra she pays.

5. PROGRAMS FOR FORMULAS

(*a*) Work through this program. What does it compute?

A	B
4	

Input to *A*.
Replace *B* by $A \times A$.
Replace *B* by $A \times B$.
Output from *B*.

What changes would have to be made in order to compute 5^3?

Check that you agree that the instructions would still be the same, and that the only change would be in the input number.

The program above will compute x^3, where x is any number, if this number x is put into store *A*.

In this section we are going to look at some more programs which can be used for formulas.

(b) An approximate formula for the area, A, of a circle of radius x is

$$A = 3x^2.$$

Figure 3 shows a flow diagram for the formula:

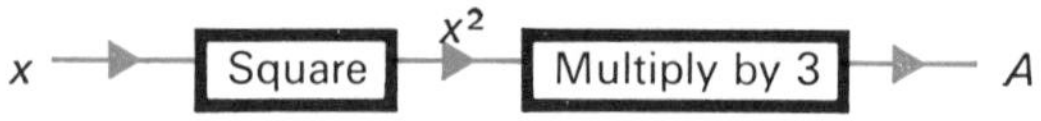

$$x \longrightarrow \boxed{\text{Square}} \xrightarrow{x^2} \boxed{\text{Multiply by 3}} \longrightarrow A$$

Fig. 3

Use this flow diagram to help you write a program for the formula. Assume that the radius x is put in store A.

(c) Work through the following program using the input x. What does it compute?

How does it differ from the program for finding the area of a circle?

A	B	C
x		

Input to A.

Replace B by $3 \times A$.

Replace C by $B \times B$.

Output from C.

(d) Work through the next program with the inputs x and y, and so obtain a formula for the output.

A	B	C	D	E
x				
	y			

Input to A.

Input to B.

Replace C by $A \times A$.

Replace D by $A \times B$.

Replace E by $C - D$.

Output from E.

Exercise B

1 Write a program to compute x^7.

2 Write a program to compute x^8 using as few instructions and stores as possible.

3 Write a program to compute $3x^2 + x$.

4   Write programs to give the following:

(a) $(x-4)^2$;   (b) x^2-4.

5   Write a program for $\dfrac{x}{y}+\dfrac{y}{x}$.

6   Write a program for $\dfrac{1}{x}+\dfrac{1}{y}$.

7   Write a program for $\dfrac{xy}{x+y}$.

8   Write programs for (a) $3x^2+3y^2$;   (b) $3(x+y)^2$.

9   Write a program to compute v where

$$v = u+at.$$

Start with inputs of u, a and t to stores A, B, C, respectively.

10   Write a program to compute s where

$$s = ut+\tfrac{1}{2}at^2.$$

6. PROGRAMS WITH LOOPS

Figure 4 shows a flow diagram which you met in the Prelude to this book (see p. 7). It is a flow diagram for multiplying 6 by 5.

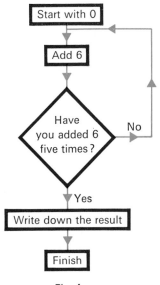

Fig. 4

In order to write a program for this flow diagram a new type of instruction is needed which can cope with the question in the diamond-shaped
box. Here is a program which will do it. Work through the program.

	A	B	C
	0		
		6	
			5

(1) Input to *A*.
(2) Input to *B*.
(3) Input to *C*.
(4) Replace *A* by *A*+*B*.
(5) Replace *C* by *C*−1.
(6) If *C* > 0, go back to
        instruction (4).

(7) Output from *A*.
(8) Finish.

Instruction (6) in this program is of a new type. It has the effect of
sending you back round the loop. The number in store *C* is reduced by
1 every time you go round the loop, until it becomes 0, and then instruction
(7) is followed.

In order to multiply 7 by 8 what changes would be needed in the input
numbers? Would there be any changes in the program?

Exercise C

1 Work through the following program. What does it do?

	A	B	C
	42		
		6	
			0

(1) Input to *A*.
(2) Input to *B*.
(3) Input to *C*.
(4) Replace *A* by *A*−*B*.
(5) Replace *C* by *C*+1.
(6) If *A* > 0, go back to
        instruction (4).

(7) Output from *C*.
(8) Finish.

2 Work through the following program. What sequence of numbers does it deal with in store *D*?

A	B	C	D
0			
	1		
		10	

(1) Input to *A*.
(2) Input to *B*.
(3) Input to *C*.
(4) Replace *D* by $A + B$.
(5) Replace *A* by *B*.
(6) Replace *B* by *D*.
(7) Replace *C* by $C - 1$.
(8) If $C > 0$, go back to instruction (4).

(9) Output from *D*.
(10) Finish.

3 Work through the next program. What sequence of numbers does it deal with in store *A*?

A	B	C
1		
	1	
		10

(1) Input to *A*.
(2) Input to *B*.
(3) Input to *C*.
(4) Replace *B* by $B + 1$.
(5) Replace *A* by $A + B$.
(6) Replace *C* by $C - 1$.
(7) If $C > 0$, go back to instruction (4).

(8) Output from *A*.
(9) Finish.

4 (*a*) Work through this program:

	A	B	C
(1) Input to *A*.	1		
(2) Input to *B*.		2	
(3) Input to *C*.			6

(1) Input to *A*.
(2) Input to *B*.
(3) Input to *C*.
(4) Replace *A* by *A* × *B*
(5) Replace *C* by *C* − 1.
(6) If *C* > 0, go back to
    instruction (4).

(7) Output from *A*.
(8) Finish.

(*b*) What modifications, if any, would be needed in order to compute
3⁵?

5 Work through the flow diagram in Figure 5 and find out what it does.
Then write a program which will output the last number of the
sequence.

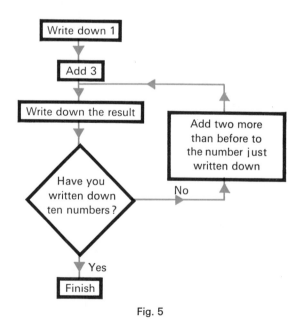

Fig. 5

6 Write a program which will output the first ten counting numbers.

7 Write a program which will output the first twenty odd numbers.

8 Invent a program of your own choice involving a loop.

Puzzle corner

1 A brass band of 40 musicians takes 4 minutes to play a march. How long would a band of 60 musicians take?

2 Fold a square from a rectangular piece of paper. Cut out the square. Now fold an equilateral triangle from the square piece of paper.

3 How can you use four 9's to represent one hundred?

4 Sally has 6 identical pairs of socks except that 3 pairs are white and 3 are beige. The 12 socks are all loose in a drawer and Sally picks them out one at a time without looking. How many must she pick out to be sure of getting a pair?

5 Can you see how the pattern in Figure 1 was formed? Notice how the circles have enveloped a square.

   Experiment to see whether you can envelop a regular hexagon with circles.

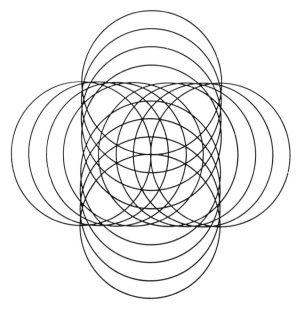

Fig. 1

6 What comes next?

(*a*) 3, 3, 6, 9, 15, 24, 39, ? ;

(*b*) 1, 5, 14, 30, 55, ? ;

(*c*) 4, 9, 25, 49, 121, ?.

7 Arrange twenty-four matches to form fourteen squares.

8 A set of dominoes (Figure 2 shows an example of one member) ranges from double zero to double six. How many different dominoes are there? How many dots are there on one set?

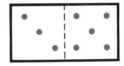

Fig. 2

9 Children often select one of their group for a game by standing in a circle and counting around the circle with the phrase:

'This year, next year, sometime, never'.

At each stage, the person corresponding to 'never' drops out. There are seven children in a circle (see Figure 3). The counting starts with '*a*' and is carried out in a clockwise direction. Who will be selected? What will happen if the counting is carried out in an anticlockwise direction?

Fig. 3

Puzzle corner

10 Trace and cut out four shapes the same as Figure 4. Arrange the pieces to form (*a*) a square, (*b*) a parallelogram.

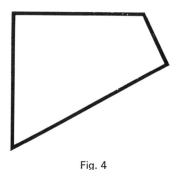

Fig. 4

11 Penny, Robin, Sarah and Tim win the first four prizes in an Art competition. In how many different ways can they have been placed?

12

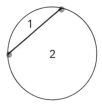 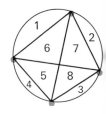

Fig. 5

When 2 points on a circle are joined, 2 regions are formed.
When 3 points on a circle are joined, 4 regions are formed.
When 4 points on a circle are joined, 8 regions are formed.

(*a*) How many regions are formed when 5 points on a circle are joined?

(*b*) How many regions are formed when 6 points on a circle are joined? (No, the answer is not 32!)

13 (*a*) Take a piece of paper about 25 cm long and 3 cm wide and stick the ends together to form a ring (see Figure 6(*a*)). Cut along the middle of the strip with a pair of scissors. What happens?

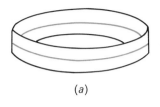 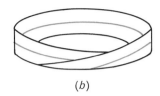

(a) (b)

Fig. 6

(b) Now take another strip of paper but before sticking the ends together, hold one end and twist the other through a half-turn (see Figure 6 (b)). Cut along the middle of this strip. What happens this time?

(c) Make a ring as you did in (b). Try to guess what will happen if you cut along it 1 cm from the edge. Now make the cut. Were you right?

(d) Experiment to see what results you can get by making rings with more twists.

14 Find the greatest number of different rectangles in each of the figures (a)–(d) in Figure 7. Copy and complete the table below. (To help you, the answers to (a) and (b) have been given.)

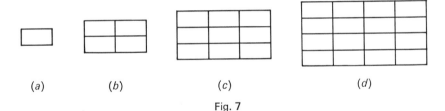

(a) (b) (c) (d)

Fig. 7

	(a)	(b)	(c)	(d)
Number of small rectangles in top row	1	2	3	4
Number of rectangles counted	1	9		

(a) Is there a pattern among the numbers? If so, explain it in your own words.

(b) How many rectangles would there be in a rectangle with five rows and five columns?

Revision exercises

Computation 5

1 $^-6 + {}^-2 - 5.$

2 $1\frac{1}{2} \times \frac{2}{3}.$

3 $0{\cdot}71 \times 12.$

4 $0{\cdot}1675 \div 25.$

5 $(12)^2 - (1{\cdot}2)^2.$

6 Find the value of $12 \times$ cosine of $25{\cdot}2°.$

Computation 6

1 $26{\cdot}05 \div 0{\cdot}45.$

2 $\sqrt{(15 \times 60)}.$

3 Simplify $\frac{1}{2} + \frac{2}{3} + \frac{3}{4}.$

4 $(98{\cdot}4 + 6{\cdot}6) \div 3{\cdot}5.$

5 15% of £840.

6 $\begin{pmatrix} 2 & {}^-1 & 0 \\ 3 & 0 & 4 \end{pmatrix} \begin{pmatrix} 1 \\ 0 \\ {}^-2 \end{pmatrix}.$

Exercise K

1 If $a = {}^-1$, $b = 1$ and $c = 0$, find the value of $a^2 + b^2 + c^2.$

2 How can you distinguish between an odd and even number in base two?

3 What is 6% of £30?

4 State the values of the following:

   (a) $\sqrt{81}$;   (b) $\sqrt{8100}$;   (c) $\sqrt{0{\cdot}09}$;   (d) $\sqrt{0{\cdot}0004}.$

5 Find the lengths of the unknown sides in Figure 1.

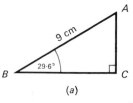

(a)

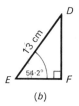

(b)

Fig. 1

6 $2(x - 3) = {}^-4.$ Find the value of $x.$

154

7 Draw a Schlegel diagram for a square-based pyramid by removing a triangular face.

8 What linear relation do the following points satisfy?

$$(0, 6), \quad (1, 5), \quad (3, 3), \quad (4. 2).$$

Exercise L

1 What is a prime number? Express 120 as a product of prime factors.

2 How many times is the volume of a sphere increased if its radius is doubled?

3 If $y = 3x - 1$, what is y when $x = {}^-3$?

4 $11011_{\text{two}} \div 11_{\text{two}}$. Give the answer in base two.

5 What is the symmetry number of a regular hexagonal prism?

6 $14 - x = {}^-2$. Find the value of x.

7 What is the final bearing after turning $170°$ clockwise from east?

8 Find the area of a triangle whose vertices are $({}^-2, 1)$, $(2, 1)$, $(0, 4)$.

Exercise M (*Multi-choice*)

In this exercise there may be more than one correct answer to a question. Write down the letter (or letters) corresponding to the correct answer (or answers). Show any rough working that you do.

1 Which of the shapes in Figure 2 are topologically equivalent to a circle?

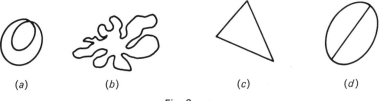

(a)   (b)   (c)   (d)

Fig. 2

2 A cuboid (rectangular box) measures 50 cm by 1 m by 10 m. Its volume is

(a) 500 cm³;   (b) 500 m³;   (c) 20 m³;   (d) 5 m³.

155

3   Which of the following statements are true about the regular triangular prism shown in Figure 3?

   (*a*) Its symmetry number is 6;

   (*b*) it has 3 axes of symmetry;

   (*c*) it has 4 planes of symmetry;

   (*d*) it has exactly 6 edges.

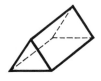

Fig. 3

4   In Figure 4, *M* and *N* are mid-points of sides of a square. The ratio of the area of the shaded triangle to the area of the complete square is

   (*a*) 1 to 8;   (*b*) 16 to 2;   (*c*) 2 to 14;   (*d*) 2 to 16.

Fig. 4

5   The vertices of a rectangle are (0, 0), (6, 0), (6, 4) and (0, 4). Which of the following are equations of the lines of symmetry of the rectangle?

   (*a*) $x = 3$;   (*b*) $y = 3$;   (*c*) $y = 2$;   (*d*) $x = 2$.

6   In Figure 5, the shaded area represents:

   (*a*) $(A \cup B) \cap C$;

   (*b*) $(A \cup C) \cap B$;

   (*c*) $A \cap (C \cup B)$;

   (*d*) $B \cap (C \cup A)$.

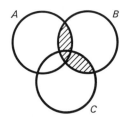

Fig. 5

Exercise N

1 Solve the following equations. (In (d), remember that $3+x$ can be written as $x+3$.)

(a) $2x-3 = 7$;　　　　　　　(b) $3(x+1) = {}^{-}6$;

(c) $7-2x = 10$;　　　　　　　(d) $\frac{1}{2}(3+x) = 3$;

(e) $4(2-x) = 6$;　　　　　　　(f) $2(\frac{1}{2}x+1) = 8$.

2 The matrix

$$\mathbf{J} = \begin{pmatrix} 1 & 4 & 2 & 1 \\ 4 & 1 & 1 & 2 \end{pmatrix}$$

shows the journeys from the origin to the vertices of the trapezium *ABCD* (see Figure 6).

(a) Multiply **J** by the matrix $\begin{pmatrix} 0 & 1 \\ -1 & 0 \end{pmatrix}$ on the left.

(b) On a copy of Figure 6, show the trapezium *ABCD* and its image after the transformation represented by

$$\begin{pmatrix} 0 & 1 \\ -1 & 0 \end{pmatrix}.$$

(c) Describe the transformation which $\begin{pmatrix} 0 & 1 \\ -1 & 0 \end{pmatrix}$ represents.

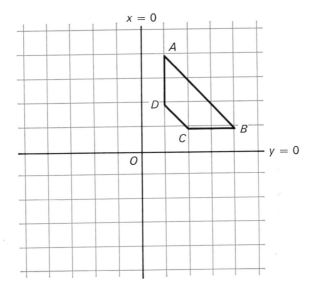

Fig. 6

3 Mary and Nancy are playing snakes and ladders with two different dice. One is a cube numbered from 0 to 5 and the other is a regular tetrahedron numbered from 0 to 3.

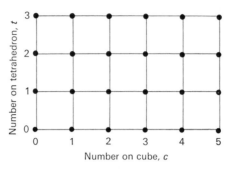

Fig. 7

Copy Figure 7. Draw a graph to show the relation $c + t = 6$.

At one stage in the game, Mary finds that a total score of 2 would send her counter down a snake and so would a total score of 6.

On the same diagram:

(*a*) Show in red all the possible scores which would result in her counter going down the first snake.

(*b*) Show in blue all the possible scores which would result in her missing both the snakes.

4 Write a program to compute the volume, V, of the triangular prism in Figure 8, where $V = \frac{1}{2}abh$. (Start with inputs of a, b and h to stores A, B, C, respectively.)

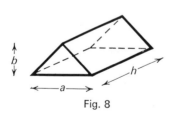

Fig. 8

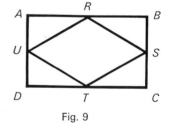

Fig. 9

5 In Figure 9, *ABCD* is a rectangle and *R*, *S*, *T*, *U* are the mid-points of the sides. $AB = 10$ cm and $BC = 8$ cm.

(*a*) What special name do we give to quadrilateral *RSTU*?

(*b*) Use Pythagoras's rule to calculate the length of *TS*.

(*c*) Use your tables to help you calculate the size of angle *STC*.

6 Use your slide rule to calculate the following. (Do not forget to make rough estimates of the answers first.)

(*a*) 38×18; (*b*) 0.84×1.5; (*c*) 4800×0.95;

(*d*) $\sqrt{1850}$; (*e*) $(40.8)^2$; (*f*) $83 \div 1.25$;

(*g*) $0.77 \div 10.2$; (*h*) $\sqrt{0.64}$; (*i*) $\dfrac{9.8 \times 2.64}{5.7}$.

Exercise O

1 Solve the following equations:

(*a*) $3x + 6 = 4$; (*b*) $\frac{1}{2}(3x - 2) = 1$; (*c*) $4 - 3x = 8$;

(*d*) $3 - \frac{1}{3}x = {}^{-}9$; (*e*) $\frac{1}{3}(2 + x) = 1\frac{1}{2}$; (*f*) $2(3 - 4x) = 5$.

2 (*a*) Write down a 2 by 4 matrix to show the journeys from the origin to *O*, *P*, *Q*, *R* (see Figure 10). Call it **J**.

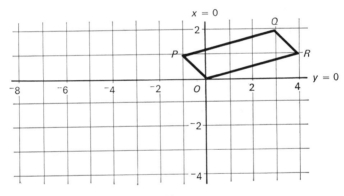

Fig. 10

(*b*) Multiply **J** by the matrix $\begin{pmatrix} -2 & 0 \\ 0 & -2 \end{pmatrix}$ on the left.

(*c*) On a diagram show the parallelogram *OPQR* and its image after the transformation represented by the matrix

$$\begin{pmatrix} -2 & 0 \\ 0 & -2 \end{pmatrix}.$$

(*d*) Describe the transformation which $\begin{pmatrix} -2 & 0 \\ 0 & -2 \end{pmatrix}$ represents.

159

3 (a) Sarah goes to the baker for her mother to buy some currant buns and some eclairs. The buns cost 2p each and the eclairs 3p each. Sarah has 30p to spend and buys b buns and e eclairs. Explain why $2b + 3e \leqslant 30$.

(b) Find three ways in which Sarah could spend all the money and use these to draw the line $2b + 3e = 30$.

(c) By shading out the unwanted region, draw a graph of Sarah's solution set. Label your graph.

(d) In how many different ways could Sarah spend only some of her money?

4 Write a program to compute

$$5 + 5^2 + 5^3.$$

Try to do it using only two store compartments.

5 James has a toy yacht which he sails diagonally across a rectangular pond 8 m long and 5 m wide. James walks round two edges of the pond to meet his yacht when it reaches the other corner.

How much further has James walked than the yacht sailed? (You need to use your slide rule for this question.)

6 Draw a sketch of a hexagonal prism and then draw a Schlegel diagram for this prism by removing

(a) a hexagonal face;

(b) a rectangular face.

Colour each Schlegel diagram using as few colours as possible, so that adjacent faces are not the same colour.

Exercise P

1 Explain how to find the sum of the angles in a pentagon by dividing it into triangles.

Hence find the value of x in Figure 11.

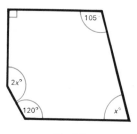

Fig. 11

2 Figure 12 shows a square-ended cuboid with a square-based pyramid fitting *exactly* on top. The top of the pyramid is over the centre of the top of the cuboid.

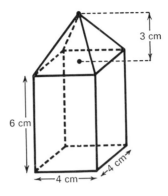

Fig. 12

(*a*) How many planes of symmetry has the figure?

(*b*) How many axes of symmetry has the figure? State the order of rotational symmetry about each axis.

(*c*) What is the symmetry number of the solid?

(*d*) The volume, *V*, of a pyramid is given by $V = \frac{1}{3}Ah$ where *A* is the area of the base and *h* is the height. Use this formula to help you find the total volume of the solid shown in Figure 12.

3 Express 1764 in prime factors and hence find its square root.

4 Make a table of values for $y = x^2 + 2x - 1$ for values of *x* between ⁻5 and 3 and draw the graph.
    Find the solutions of:

(*a*) $x^2 + 2x - 1 = 7$;

(*b*) $x^2 + 2x - 1 = {}^-2$.

5 How can you recognize an even number if it is written in

(*a*) base two;

(*b*) base three?

6 p is the set of points of one circle and q is the set of points of the other and $p \cap q = \{A, B\}$. (See Figure 13.)

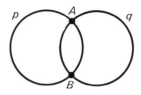

Fig. 13

The number of elements in $p \cap q$ is 2. We can write this as

$$n(p \cap q) = 2.$$

Draw two circles to illustrate each of the following. If it is impossible to draw a particular diagram, say so.

(*a*) $n(p \cap q) = 0$;

(*b*) $n(p \cap q) = 1$;

(*c*) $n(p \cap q) = 3$.

Exercise Q

1 On squared paper, mark axes with values of x and y between $^-4$ and 4. Draw the triangle whose vertices have coordinates (2, 3), (3, 1), (2, 1). Label it T.

T can be mapped onto a triangle, S, by a translation with vector

$$\begin{pmatrix} -4 \\ -2 \end{pmatrix}.$$

Draw and label S.

S can be mapped onto another triangle, R, by a translation with vector $\begin{pmatrix} 3 \\ -2 \end{pmatrix}$. Draw and label R.

(*a*) What single translation would map T onto R?

(*b*) Explain why it is impossible to find a single reflection which would map T onto R.

(*c*) Explain why it is impossible to find a single rotation which would map T onto R.

2 $\frac{3}{50}$ can be written as a terminating decimal because its bottom number can be divided exactly into 10^2 which is a power of ten.

$\frac{5}{33}$ cannot be written as a terminating decimal because 33 will not divide exactly into any power of 10.

Without working them out, say which of the following fractions can be written as recurring decimals:

(a) $\frac{11}{30}$;　　　(b) $\frac{17}{40}$;　　　(c) $\frac{4}{25}$;　　　(d) $\frac{19}{32}$;

(e) $\frac{1}{41}$;　　　(f) $\frac{7}{80}$;　　　(g) $\frac{4}{81}$;　　　(h) $\frac{33}{125}$.

3

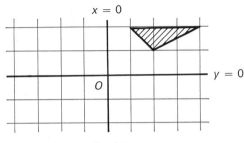

Fig. 14

Copy Figure 14 onto squared paper and use it to help you complete the following operation table. (Some entries have been made to help you.)

I stands for the identity (or stay-put) transformation;

H stands for a rotation through a half-turn about O;

X stands for a reflection in $x = 0$;

Y stands for a reflection in $y = 0$.

	Followed by	Second transformation			
		I	H	X	Y
	I			X	
First transformation	H				
	X		Y		
	Y				I

Use your table to find the inverse of

(a) H;　　　　　(b) Y;　　　　　(c) X.

4　Poker dice have on their faces an ace, a king, a queen, a jack, a ten and a nine. If 2 dice are thrown, what is the probability that the following will occur?

(a) 2 tens;

(b) 2 pictures (that is, a king, queen or jack);

(c) 1 ace and 1 king.

5   A model of an aircraft is built on a scale of 1 to 32. Use your slide rule to complete a copy of the following table.

	Model	Aircraft
Length of wing	0·5 m	
Length of fuselage	0·38 m	
Height of tail		4·5 m

6   Every square number is either a multiple of 3 or is one more than a multiple of 3. Give one example of each kind.

Write down the first twelve square numbers and underneath each one write *M* if it is a multiple of 3 and *N* if it is one more than a multiple of 3. You should notice a pattern among the *M*'s and *N*'s. By considering differences, try to explain why the pattern occurs.

Exercise R

Copy and complete this cross-number.

Clues across

1. How many sixths in $2\frac{1}{2}$?
3. 2^5.
5. The mean of 1230, 1235, 1236, 1239, 1240.
9. The sum of the numbers in the seventh row of Pascal's triangle.
11. $\sqrt{6400}$.
12. The sum of the prime factors of 210.
13. $50 \times$ sine of $55 \cdot 1°$.
15. 101_{six} in base ten.
16. $19 \cdot 9 + {}^-4 \cdot 8 + 3 \cdot 4 - 0 \cdot 5$.
17. The fifth prime number.
18. The half-way value of the group 40–52.
19. $V = a^2 - b^2 - 1$. What is V when $a = 6$ and $b = {}^-3$?
21. $237 \cdot 9 \div 3 \cdot 9$.
23. 15_{eight} in binary.
25. $£0 \cdot 11\frac{1}{2} + £0 \cdot 34 + £0 \cdot 29\frac{1}{2}$ in pence.
26. $75 \times$ cosine of $36 \cdot 6°$ to 2 s.f.

Clues down

2. The median of 50, 49, 54, 46, 52, 55.
3. The sixth square number.
4. $A = (a+3)^2$. What is A when $a = {}^-9$?
6. The seventh triangle number.
7. The number of degrees in one-third of a right-angle.
8. 1, 3, 4, 7, 11, 18, 29, ?.
10. $(18 \cdot 4 \times 24) \div 0 \cdot 1$.
12. The volume in cm³ of a cuboid measuring 11 cm by 12 cm by 13 cm.
14. $\sqrt{324}$.
15. $^-4, ^-1, 4, 11, 20, ?$.
18. If $\frac{1}{2}x - 3 = 17$, what is x?
19. Three angles of a quadrilateral are each $113°$. What is the size (in degrees) of the fourth angle?
20. 16% of 375.
22. $3 \cdot \dot{3} + 6 \cdot \dot{6}$.
23. The number of one-nodes in the word THREE.
24. The symmetry number of a regular octagonal prism.